To Fill the Unforgiving Minute

To Fill the Unforgiving Minute

Donald Patrick Foster

iUniverse, Inc.
New York Lincoln Shanghai

To Fill the Unforgiving Minute

All Rights Reserved © 2003 by Donald Patrick Foster

No part of this book may be reproduced or transmitted in any form or by any means, graphic, electronic, or mechanical, including photocopying, recording, taping, or by any information storage retrieval system, without the written permission of the publisher.

iUniverse, Inc.

For information address:
iUniverse, Inc.
2021 Pine Lake Road, Suite 100
Lincoln, NE 68512
www.iuniverse.com

ISBN: 0-595-28932-0 (pbk)
ISBN: 0-595-65940-3 (cloth)

Printed in the United States of America

In memory of my beloved parents, Frances and Patrick O'Sullivan Foster and our beloved children, Suzanne and Timothy O'Sullivan Foster, who are watching from above.

Dedicated to my loving wife, Anne, being by my side for these past 45 years, who has been my inspiration. I wrote a poem to her on Christmas last that senses my feelings and it goes—What greater love hath any woman to give her life, her essence for her children and soul mate.

My love, yours is of undying spirit and unconditional love—your giving, your compassion is beyond one's worldly know so pure—so complete, it is as if before time began your fate.

Your radiant smile lights up your being from the inside and out, as part of your boundless energy flow. My Sunshine, my very being has been so vastly enriched by your life. You and you alone are the binding force of my soul,—my ultimate life's quest of knowing you and your being—you—mother, wife and best friend. My darling, my Anne, my wife to life's end. *When one finds a worthy wife her value is far beyond pearls. Her husband entrusts his heart to her, he has an unfailing prize. She brings him good and not evil all the days of his life. Proverbs 10:10*

Dedicated to all the wonderful smells, feelings, memories, places been and people known, this celebration of life is at the water's edge trees and mountains in the foreground, with good music, good talk on any day, but best on a fall, winter-like day.

May the road rise to meet you, May the wind always be at your back and may the sun shine warmly on your face and the rainfall softly upon your fields and may God always hold you in the hollow of His hand. This Irish prayer is my approach to having God help me to live a full and rich life.

Thank you again my beloved Mother and Father for the wonderful genes that have come my way.

Contents

Prologue 1

Part I: Reflections on Life 3

Part II: Contradictions and the Game 5

Part III: Genes and Environment—Gleanings of Life 14

Part IV: Tapestry and Your Life 21

Part V: Essence of Life's Journey and Its Insights 26

Part VI: Thinking and Living A Fuller Life 30

Part VII: Dynamics of Life's Investments 37

Part VIII: Life's Challenge—Dyadics of Relationships 44

Part IX: Times of My Life and Civil Disobedience 55

Part X: Deep, Deep Reflections 68

Part XI: Karma of People and Thinking 71

Part XII: Looking Back Again 75

Part XIII: Reflections 80

Part XIV: Lifetime of Gleanings—Living on the Edge 84

Epilogue 93

Acknowledgements

To my wife for her love, loyalty, compassion, beauty and being my best friend.

To my mother and father for their exemplary life, and the love and wisdom they gave me.

To my sister for her love and steadfastness and being the best sister a brother could have.

To all my children for their inner beauty and goodness.

To my father's brother for unwittingly introducing me at age 5 to his girlfriends with whom I had my first taste of affection outside of kin.

To the executor of my mother's estate who gave me the knowledge of knowing who my relatives are, as Will Rogers said.

Thanks to my childhood friends, Donnie and Bill, and all the rest who made my childhood a wonderful adventure.

Thanking my doctor "friend" for showing me who he was after beating him in tennis by never speaking to me again and canceling all of the insurance I had sold him. Thank God it was better to have learned, then, what I was up against than later to "learn!"

Thanks to my high school basketball coach, Ray, for taking my challenge to play the basketball team with a few friends from the playground, Peppy, George, Pat and Jim, and beating the school team. It was my affirmation of independence and confidence.

'Thanks to my friends, Bob and John, who have gone to the other side for the fun times and living thru me vicariously in my adventures with life and the law.

Lastly, thanks to God for giving me the cerebral ability to live on the edge. It has been an adventure!

Prologue

In the film *Shenandoah*, Jimmy Stewart says, "If we don't try we won't do and if we don't do, what are we here on earth for?"

Rudyard Kipling, the English poet wrote just before he died, the poem *If* in the last stanza is an important thought; "If you can fill the unforgiving minute with sixty seconds' worth of distance run, yours is the earth and everything that is in it and which is more—you'll be a man my son."

Anything we ardently desire, honestly believe, and expectantly act toward will inevitably come to pass. Life is a kaleidoscope of interesting people, places, thoughts, smells, sights and feelings. When we love and give love we begin to divide ourselves; this multiplies our being. We find ourselves by giving ourselves away and only then do we realize the beauty of people, places and things. Life moves oh so quickly that if you are not in love with life you are dead because your passions have gone to steel. You must ask yourself every day "Are you satisfied with the way you are trading your time?"

It was snowing at 7:10 AM January 26, 1935. Ironically it is that same white snow on the ground at 7:10 AM January 26, 2002. Memories of the circuses, the baseball games, the playground where I played are fresh in my mind. Many times I have wanted to go back to the neighborhood where I grew up and feel the thoughts and bring the memories of people, smells, tastes and experiences back to life.

February 9, 1957, my wonderful wife, Anne, and I were married. I have been taking notes, thinking thoughts and feeling feelings on my life over these years that have motivated me to create a book to be an anthology of events, thoughts, observations and places I have been and people I have known. "Be aggressive with each day—gather ye rosebuds while ye may" has synergized in my approach to life. Of late, I have been more aware of what I do with my time, wondering what others do with their time and resources.

Once, many years ago, I read an epitaph that mirrors my philosophy: "A master in the art of living who draws no sharp distinction between his education or his recreation, his work or his play leaves others to determine whether he is working or playing because to himself he is always doing both". It is this philosophy that makes life an exciting journey.

Part I:
Reflections on Life

How important! To be happy and fulfilled by our daily lives no matter how humble they may be? A completeness of living is to be good to yourself.

Salvadore Dali, the great Spanish surrealistic artist, could paint man's journey in bigger than life on canvas of how he lived, where he went and with whom he associated. This being a reflection of how man feels and thinks, of how he thought as a child, honed as he ages, in his life's work.

In my mid 20's to mid 40's, I had an energy level that knew no limits—like a wild horse always at full speed, not harnessed nor focused. By choice or chance I was told, "You are a rogue, you live on the brink of disaster and love every second of it." I understood then, as well as now, to take in the reins to maximize the moments left on earth.

Beginning the decade of my 50s the unforgiving minute has accelerated, it has been like a few months, becoming increasingly aware of how I invest money, time, thoughts and energy. The apex of life and living has been to reach. Cervantes said, "The journey is more important than the inn." If we cannot keep our balance and widen the inverted V of living, we will fall and the fall can be fatal. The Chinese have taught us to keep a balance between the ying and the yang.

I imagine what the day will to be, what is going to be said and to whom, eliciting feelings, reactions, and thinking. Enriching one's life is to give one's self a broader insight, to deepen love and understanding.

The philosophical realizations that have charmed my life, luck, and others were borne out of intuitive feelings. The first is marrying my wife on February 9, 1957, as the most important day of my life. Secondly, moving into a house with no mortgage payment for five years in an upscale area of Virginia Beach. By negotiating with the developer on growth of the equity—the house itself doubling in value (1969–1974)—we settled on the home for a token amount of monies. I could afford it the least when needing it the most. Now it is a pleasant retreat for family and friends.

Thirdly, going in the life insurance business in June 1956, becoming the youngest member of the Million Dollar Round Table in the world. (The MDRT: an international organization of the world's top salesmen selling life insurance). The networking this provided, worldwide, has been rewarding and has added to my personal growth.

Fourth facet of good fortune has been having a proclivity toward exercise and the psychological challenges that honed me by having a gargantuan appetite for life.

Fifth in life's priorities is having developed a highly sensitive awareness of how wonderful are the things of nature: sun, rain, air, the trees, greenery, whitecap mountains and the oceans that are about us. It is difficult sometimes to fulfill yourself in this area unless you are at peace with yourself.

Lastly and probably the most important, is being alive, aware and consumed with passion. Thanking God daily for the blessings that He has given me and letting me pass them on. Hoping that it might be said that the world is a better place to live because I passed this way.

Part II:
Contradictions and the Game

A: Medicine

Jean Francois Revel, the French philosopher, states in his book, *Flight From Truth—the Reign of Deceit,* that we live in an age of lies. The wealth of information in all fields and the people who enjoy rapid and easy access to information is unparalleled in human history. Foremost of all forces that drive the world is falsehood. For example, the amount of people who have been injured and killed by unnecessary surgery, to medicines prescribed, to staph infections is mind-boggling. Dr. Norman Mallick, a 1992 nominee for the Nobel Prize in medicine, states that 300,000 people were killed in hospitals in that year. This is more than those who died in WWII, Korea and Viet Nam combined.

Hospitals are somewhat like the book, later made into a movie, *Soylent Green,* which portrays an overflow of people on earth who are fed by the less fortunate. The scene is presented where for once in the poor person's life he is treated with respect and dignity and is privileged with beautiful panoramic views, a tasteful dinner and heavenly music before he is poisoned with the wine and turned into a cookie to feed the rich.

Sometimes the cure often is where the problem is. The practice of medicine is literally killing the patient, as many die from the cure. Voltaire, a physician/philosopher, was exiled by the French government over two centuries ago for his too-honest approach, "physicians prescribe medicines they know little about for diseases they know less about to patients they know nothing about." Leonardo DaVinci, probably one of the greatest minds that ever lived, was highly critical of the physicians of his day—destroyers of life are physicians because taking drugs are a form of alchemy. "He who takes medicines is ill-advised."

Iatrogenic disease (physician caused disease) is a pioneer in the demise of man and keeping in mind it's the person who must be treated—not the disease. The holistic approach to curing is helping the mind with the body and de-emphasizing invasive and heavy prescriptive medicine, holistic medicine is still in its infancy.

Annual physical exams are often a health risk. Hospitals are dangerous places for the sick. Most operations do little good and many do harm. Medical testing laboratories are scandalously inaccurate. Many drugs cause more problems than they cure. X-ray machines are the most pervasive and most dangerous tool in the doctor's office. These words are from a respected physician, Robert Mendelsohn, MD, professor of preventive medicine at the School of Medicine, University of Illinois. Most doctors are unable to recognize wellness because they are not trained in wellness, but rather disease. In 1973 physicians went on strike in the Los Angeles, CA area for the better part of a year resulting in a dramatic decrease in patient mortality.

When I grew up in the 1940s, almost all children had a tonsillectomy and a $500 Metropolitan life insurance policy. Now they are rarely done, as they were unnecessary. It is said now among physicians jokingly, "By the age of 50, if you don't have a pacemaker you are not in the in-crowd." An angioplasty, which is usually over-committed, has a life of approximately seven years. Hospitals' dust and dirt are not the kind of dust and dirt you find anywhere else. Where else can you find in one building animal, vegetable and biological waste, catheters, bodily secretions, syringes and fecal material all of which is going down the same chute collected and disposed by the same people who have access to the patients' rooms as well as the kitchen, laboratory and the morgue.

Linus Pauling, Nobel Prize winner in medicine, was deprived of funds by the National Cancer Institute to find out if ascorbic acid provided benefit for cancer patients, which his earlier research concluded.

What is needed is a new medicine, a new vision of medical cure, which makes the physician a guardian of health care, diminishing his need and becoming more aware of nutritional therapy, acupuncture, kineseology and homeopathic medicine. New medical school would have a department of iatrogenic disease so that the art of medicine may surpass the science of medicine.

B: Economics

Remembering as a child, asking my grandfather why it took ten people to do one person's work? To me it seemed like it would add to a company's problems, a nation's problems as somebody somehow was going to have to pay for this. In my 20s a tennis friend, an engineering co-op student in a local shipyard, observed that 10 people were doing the work of one and being paid for it, remembering he called it work done by osmosis. (Where enough people look at the work and finally it gets done, working to stretch work to fill the time.) Understanding the *Peter Principle*, a book written in the1960s, shows how one rises to his level of incompetence, a grandchild of this process of osmosis. Unfortunately when carelessness and incompetence become rampant in the workplace it spills into other worlds of endeavor and increasingly we become exposed to harm's way.

For example, the economic scenario is wrought with the manipulation of supply and demand whether in the marketplace or the government establishment. In the book *Marketing Warfare* it is pointed out that hamburgers, automobiles and homes can be made better at a far less cost. John Ruskin's statement, "There is nothing that was ever made that cannot be made cheaper with more cost to the consumer," is somewhat of an oxymoron. The recent corporate accounting fiascos are perfect examples of a 1920's Ponzi scheme with the government, the executive corporate management in white-collar conspiracy.

In the arena tens of millions of dollars are spent for political campaigns—appealing to the populace with many promises. Win them with honest trivia and betray them in deepest consequence. Charles

McKay's book, *The Madness of the Crowd and Other Popular Delusions*, can be seen in this controlled insanity—from the tulip mania 300 years ago to the tech market of the recent decade. This book with its theme that most people wind up years later with a lot of good stories and no money, certainly depicts the vacuum in the political/economic arena and the waste that fuels it. Bernard Baruch said, "We never would have had a depression if man understood that two plus two equals four." We find man's tendency to strike at the Achilles heel of other men an ideal format to deceive and to increase the coffers of many a pseudo "do-gooder." Seemingly everyone wants a cause to follow and to believe. The book *True Believers* by Eric Hoffer, shows that revolutions, whether theological or ideological, begin one way and eventually move 180 degrees out, again man manipulating man.

The following: Food for Thought has been carried in my briefcase for the last forty years and brings me to the essence of being alive.

In 1923, a very important meeting was held at the Edgewater Beach Hotel in Chicago. Attending this meeting were nine of the world's most successful financiers. Those present were:

The president of the largest independent steel company;

The president of the largest utility company;

The president of the largest gas company;

The greatest wheat speculator;

The president of the New York Stock Exchange;

A member of the president's cabinet;

The greatest "bear" in Wall Street

The head of the world's greatest monopoly;

The president of the Bank of International Settlement.

Certainly we must admit that here were gathered a group of the world's most successful men. At least, men who had found the secret of "making money." Let's see what happened to these men:

The president of the largest independent steel company—Charles Schwab—died a bankrupt and lived on borrowed money for five years before his death.

Albert Fall, a member of the president's cabinet, was recently pardoned from prison so that he could die at home.

The president of the greatest utility company—Samuel Insull—died a fugitive from justice and penniless in a foreign land.

Ivar Kruger, president of the Bank of International Settlements, died a suicide.

The president of the largest gas company—Howard Hopson—died insane.

Leon Fraser, head of the world's greatest monopoly, died a suicide.

The greatest wheat speculator—Arthur Cutton—died abroad—insolvent.

Richard Whitney, president of the New York Stock Exchange, died in the penitentiary.

All of these men knew the secret of making money, but not one knew how to live.

C: Judicial

The judicial system, with its pomp and circumstance, is cloaked with guilt and often a clever manipulation of rhetoric for the prosecution to outwit the defense or vice-versa. Finding underneath justice is warped with injustice of man's injustice to man. The words innocence and guilt of a certain accused have little to do with his innocence or guilt. Mockery of a system that advocates honor yet aligns itself at times to dishonorable choices. Oath taking by defendant, witnesses and plaintiff is often an orchestrated ploy. Continuances and appeals are out of a Shakespearean play, as in King Henry VIII, who was betrothed to Jane Seymour. One of the lords in the kingdom being smitten with Jane and sheepishly asking her what would the king do if he discovered this alienation of affection. She replies, "your head." Jane wisely tells him to tell the king that he can make his horse talk because within the year, perhaps the king will die or perhaps you will die or perhaps the horse will talk. The wisdom of this is another facet of the game for continuance, appeals, buying time.

In the early 60's there was a series of books written by a well-known psychiatrist, Eric Berne; Games People Play, Sex Games People Play, Political Games People Play, and Games Your Analyst Plays. These books have an underlying message: the contradictions that take on the many shapes and form whether it is judicial, spiritual, economic, sexual, political, legal, or medical.

Forty-three years ago I gave a talk entitled, "*Looking Through the Looking Glass.*" The last few lines reflect a thought from a talk heard when first entering the insurance business: "A man was looking for another man on the left bank of Paris when he saw this man checking into a hotel. However, not sure if the man was registered there, he asked if he himself was registered, to his amazement he was told that he was registered in room 20. He went to the room and knocked, the door opened and he saw a man who looked very much like himself—a little older, a little grayer and a little more dissipated. Of course he was seeing himself 30 years from now. I hope that you will like what you see 30 years from now. Understanding and having an awareness of what is going on about us and to us we make a difference. Caveat emptor is alive and well! Unfortunately often we have found the enemy and it is us (Pogo). It is a matter of paying attention.

The mathematical equation of life expressed simply and articulately in Sun Tzu's *Art of War*: To know self and others you will win a million battles—to know neither, you are destined to lose all embattlements. As in *Plutarch's Lives*, it is said that times change but men don't change. Above all to thine own self be true.

The art of Zen teaches us that life is becoming more of a person. We are the sum total of all our thoughts as Ralph Waldo Emerson said, "We are what we think about all day long."

Use of never and always is a perfect paradox in our thought makeup—there is no absolute. Our use of imagination, good people, good books, produces good thinking which in turn creates good results. As my mother so often said, "the happiest person is the one who thinks the most interesting thoughts." "Life is a mirror of king & slave—'tis just what we are and do—So give the world the best that you have and the best will come back to you. Life was given for us to use—when it makes us tired and blue, we are letting it use us instead—a foolish thing to do." When we take time to strengthen our roots, we will live longer and better lives. Thoughts of long ago, that I read and share with you.

Philosophy of Life:

Take time to think thoughts, they are a source of power

Take time to play, play is the source of perpetual youth

Take time to read—reading is the fountain of wisdom

Take time to pray—prayer can bring you more than this world ever dreamed

Take time to love—love is what makes life wonderful

Take time to laugh—laughter is the music of the soul

Many years ago there was a radio program that came on Sunday evenings called "*The Shadow*". Orson Welles was the original "Shadow." The opening line was "Who knows what evil lurks in the hearts of men—only the shadow knows." We have witnessed how this has transcended the centuries from the tulip mania two centuries ago to the most recent Heaven's Gate episode of the people committing suicide to join the spacecraft behind the comet, Hale-Bopp.

Pondering the imponderable is when we analyze past happenings such as the Ponzi scheme at the turn of the century, Adolph Hitler's ravaging Europe to Jim Jones mass homicide in Guyana. The mind, whether it is focused in political obsession, religious obsession or criminal addiction as in the case of rape, burglary, murder, we see the unleashed power of the mind when not harnessed can cause irreparable harm.

Eric Fromm's book, *Art of Loving*, tells us about maternal love, brotherly love, sexual love and love of a friend. A love that I felt for my mother and father was suppressed because of my embarrassment to say the words "I love you" so much of my life. By not expressing myself, deep feelings of love were discounted.

Behooving one to pay attention to our encounters, our thoughts and feelings as we learn from experiences if we don't; we are bound to our past. Thinking back upon my mother's death and my uncle being the executor of her estate, not realizing that he would deposit the cash proceeds in a non-interest bearing account until I corrected him. Charging my sister and myself the maximum executor's fee. Approaching him, realizing he had egg on his face, his response was "if you hadn't bothered me with your fancy lawyer friends, (my wife called him once) I wouldn't have charged anything." When I asked him why he took from my sister, as she had said nothing, his response was, "get out of my house." Fortunately or unfortunately, this was the last time we spoke. Hearing what Will Rogers once said, "You begin to know your relatives when you share an inheritance" rings true.

Listening over the years, you begin cognitively to be aware that schism and inequities are rampant whether it is an inexperienced executor or an experienced one such as a bank or other corporate fiduciary, man's incompetence and unfortunately his intellectual dishonesty. This schism runs deep and wide among family members and strikes at the roots of friendship, trust and goodwill that the perpetrator or "executor" brings forth. The real truth only known by the principals involved—what a shame for all. It reminds me of the future problems of the unborn generations in Croatia and the Balkans fighting each other over what generations did before them.

As a child, I recall my father repeatedly saying "beware the Ides of March (March 15). Patrick O'Sullivan Foster, my father, died on March 15, 1979 and his funeral was March 17, 1979—St. Patrick's Day. My father was the kindest person I ever knew. He had a most positive impact on my life as someone I respected. On this same day, another male figure in my life, William T. Earls, whom I respected, died at approximately the same time after completing a talk ironically titled "*The Last Hurrah*" and he was buried on the same St. Patrick's Day.

A past chairman of the Million Dollar Round Table, Bill Earls, was the ultimate upgrading influence of my business career. Mr. Earls and I, in the summer of 1963, had a one-on-one talk that lasted over three hours in Ft. Lauderdale, FL where he was the guest speaker at an insurance business meeting with 100 people in attendance. Our conversation was interesting to the two of us it was as if no other person was in the room. This event became a rock in a foundation of my learning experiences.

Part III: Genes and Environment—Gleanings of Life

Man has many contradictions in his makeup. The never/always principle seems to be a foundation of paradoxical thinking. For example, when one says, "I never will do that" or "I always will do that," it usually means they will do that or in the case of always, will not do that.

Observe how one purchases an item of clothing or a food staple only when it is rock bottom price, but at the same time pay thousands more for a boat, car, or home than need be. Sometimes we will purchase things at inordinately high prices because money is not an object. The joy of having is quite disproportionate to its economic value and perceived worth.

When we concede that perceptions are in the eyes of the beholder, we are awe struck in how this perception can be so far amok from what is logical, reasonable and real. We can understand how malleable the mind is when we study revolutions, which usually do a 180 degree turn, since the beginning of time. The human mind seemingly is the last unexplored continent.

This is a contradiction to the individual who says he has no money, cannot save and can hardly make ends meet as he exchanges this thinking for one that gives him immediate satisfaction. The singular truth of the above is that many individuals will pay the higher price for the same item side by side. The reason for this is that the higher price appeals to one's psyche like childhood make believe games in which we participated. There must be, he thinks subconsciously some intrinsic value to this item that no one else knows.

The dyadic blend of win-win situations is the only situation to have. It creates beauty in male-female relationships and ongoing relationships between nations. Oil and water mix causes people and nations to go to war, love to go sour, causes businesses to flounder and flowers to die. Day-to-day relationships with people are a level of good feeling, trust and excitement. Knowing sometimes not why relevant feelings are encountered with irrelevant ones and congruent thoughts with incongruent thoughts. This causes static in communication and frustrations. The best way to get more is to give more. The book written in the early 70s, *The Art of Selfishness*, by David Seabury, is an in-depth study of the machinations of the mind and selfishness brought to an unselfish level by the giving and taking of thoughts. Thinking of the lyrics Elton John's, *Funeral for a Friend*—"As I sit here in my ivory tower as the hearse goes by, I care not who and I care not why"—this is the intuitive feeling I have of my oldest daughter who is most personable, however detached. The other two younger daughters are paragons in vigor, compassion and love. The sons have a detached relationship with their families and an attitude of independence and individuality. The second son stands in exception of this; his is a binding force within his own family and has a balance that is serving him well for a happy personal and family life.

High in my thoughts is that all humans are primarily positioned by their genetic makeup. Environment gives shape to their attitudes, feeling, realizing that doing for others is an indirect way of doing for self. The wonderful feeling of doing for another cannot match in any other way.

When I was in my 30s, knowing that I would make it after all, I remembered the line from Mary Tyler Moore's TV show in the '70s. I put mental and physical demands on myself that gave me a chance to live by my wits, thriving on the brink of disaster—mentally, financially and business-wise, most of the time, loving the challenge of it all.

It is a little known fact that what is one man's meat is another man's poison—whether in a courtroom, hospital, or business. Proper mental chemistry between human beings involved—such as doctor-patient, attorney-client, husband-wife—is of a certain makeup and is powerful in accomplishing the desired results. However, change the players and an obvious win can be a loss.

A board of directors for my thinking has been there for more than half-century, consisting of my mother, father, my best friend, my worst enemy, my sports idol, my favorite aunt and cousin. Becoming older, the board would enlarge to include my beloved wife, my insurance mentors and peers around the nation as well as the lay head of the Episcopal Church. Knowing these people personally, I was able to know their thinking in decisions that I would make in personal and business life and a permeating theme of guidance aligning myself with the fabulous poem, *IF* by Rudyard Kipling, instilled in my thoughts by my mother.

As you peel back the onionskin layer by layer, you discover more and arrive at the essence of where your thoughts are. Thinking back to the 60s to the present I have kept a dossier on the ten best people, best situations, best clients, best thoughts, best places been, and best things I have seen, heard, tasted and smelled. My close friend, Dr. Thomas Voshell, who is in his mid eighties and one of those foremost ten, told me this day he is suspected of having cancer of the prostate and is bedridden with much pain. He said I was one of the reasons that he wanted to live because I cared and I was much on his mind. He mentioned that I was not an ordinary person but one who was way ahead of his time in his thinking. Our conversations over the years have been invaluable, lasting for as long as six and seven hours, discussing a wide spectrum of topics, from medicine to philosophy. The other day he was introduced to my most valuable player of 1991, a young surgeon on the staff of the Portsmouth Naval Hospital, by the name of John Newman. In many ways it reminds me of another young John, who became the assistant Surgeon General, in a similar meeting of two doctor friends named John and Tom, a cardiologist, 33 years ago. They have given me insight into myself: who I am and how to pursue a more definitive course of maximizing the minutes, days, months and years. Keeping in mind as taught in Zen, the way to maximize feeling, and life itself is to do, from time to time, things you don't normally do or don't like to do. Making us do better in the things we like to do and also expands one's 24 hours a day.

The passion of having gargantuan appetites in the areas of learning, thinking having, doing, loving, giving intensifies enjoyment of life for others as well as yourself. The example created here is contagious and intensifies your value here on earth as well as bringing out the best in others.

As we all are God's creatures we know not why we react to certain people in certain ways and respond to others in a manner that is not congruous, at times, to the person they are as well as we are. For example, we don't want to go to a certain place or do a certain thing with one person: however, we are anxious to do same with another. Many times there is no rhyme or reason for this behavior.

It is better to sleep and wake up twenty years later than to go through life always asleep—this is not living. As Benjamin Franklin said 250 years ago, "Your greatest resource is time and time is money so invest it wisely." Invest in people and the dividends received will be invaluable, in the good feelings experienced and the lessons learned, feeling that what you are and what you are capable of being is the only end in life. My thinking is best when I reflect on my "Board of Directors"—the ten most powerful human forces that have come my way over these past 40 years that have been a catalyst to richer thinking and living.

Being aware that we all are products of our genes, environment and associations is paramount in guiding us to make proper choices in our selection of what we do and how we do it. The age old thought, only for the grace of God go I or only for the grace of God there I go. I heard these words echoed by LSU psychologist, Ed Timmons, 40 years ago at a Million Dollar Round Table conference. Whether you are the richest, most learned person on earth or the poorest or physically and mentally suppressed, the question I often ponder is are we part of predestination or God's Divine Plan? The books we read and the people we know reflect our thinking and feeling. Tai Chi, which is a force of energy, has been used by the Chinese for thousands of years. It means to be in harmony with nature and our own life force. Taoism, which means the way—just is—is practiced as a religion and a way of life by millions of people. When we apply these principles to our daily lives we become richer and happier.

Franz Lizst, the Austrian composer, music instilled in me an appreciation of gentle breezes and thundering clouds as these dynamics show us who we are. Tom Watson, the former chairman of the board of IBM, said 30 years ago that all selling would be done on dyadic relationships by the 21st century (intermental chemistry). All relationships, both good and bad, have this makeup. Synergetic effects can result for bad and for good. The mind is the last unexplored continent, is a fascination and curious driven thought to learn more, be more alive. Understand your priorities and focus in for enriching your life.

To fill the unforgiving minute from the last stanza of Rudyard Kipling's poem, *IF*, sums up a lifetime of thought and feeling to me. It has influenced by attitudes, my view of the world and its people. The line, "If you can fill the unforgiving minute with 60 seconds worth of distance run, yours is the earth and everything that is in it and which is more, you'll be a man, my son." This is an ounce of words with a pound of thought.

It is fortunate for me that I know by heart the poem, *IF*. Thanks to my mother, I memorized it when I was ten years old.

IF

> If you can keep your head when all about you
> Are losing theirs and blaming it on you,
> If you can trust yourself when all men doubt you,

But make allowance for their doubting too;
If you can wait and not be tired by waiting,
Or being lied about, don't deal in lies,
Or being hated, don't give way to hating,
And yet don't look too good, nor talk too wise:
If you can dream—and not make dreams your master;
If you can think—and not make thoughts your aim;
If you can meet with Triumph and Disaster
And treat those two impostors just the same;
If you can bear to hear the truth you've spoken
Twisted by knaves to make a trap for fools,
Or watch the things you gave your life to, broken,
And stoop and build 'em up with worn-out tools:
If you can make one heap of all your winnings
And risk it on one turn of pitch-and-toss,
And lose, and start again at your beginnings
And never breathe a word about your loss;
If you can force your heart and nerve and sinew
To serve your turn long after they are gone,
And so hold on when there is nothing in you
Except the Will which says to them: "Hold on!"
If you can talk with crowds and keep your virtue,
Or walk with Kings—nor lose the common touch,
If neither foes nor loving friends can hurt you,
If all men count with you, but none too much;
If you can fill the unforgiving minute
With sixty seconds' worth of distance run,
Yours is the Earth and everything that's in it,
And—which is more-you'll be a Man, my son!

There is nothing on earth more important than filling the unforgiving minute—to be alive with thought, love and passion. The meaning of the words was so powerful in my building block that its impact has never dulled through trying times.

The years and decades have passed, this year being the eight-year of my sixth decade, the first 10 years seemed to be like 100 years ago, the last 10 years have seemed like a winter ago. It has been my experience that the last 20 minutes of a social event, business deal, political election or athletic event, the essence of life itself, is in this time period. The phrase, to love and to be loved, makes for happiness.

Part IV:
Tapestry and Your Life

Interestingly, if you know one's religion and understand his belief system you know more about the man. The book, *Religions of Man,* by Houston Smith, gives a keen insight into the comparative religions to help me with this thinking. When you know a person's friends, the books he reads and the music he likes, you have an insight into his heart. Franz Lizst, the great classical composer, could use softness and thunder interchangeably, which is symbolic in the passions of war, love and thinking. The legendary song of John Lennon of the Beatles, *Imagine,* his last song before his death, is an insight into this unfilled peace and beauty of the world and man.

Certain things thought, owned, tasted, heard as a child give full reflection and measure to self, as one gets older. Games like monopoly and checkers are like life itself showing how we feel, love and play. Remembering my playground acquaintances, there was the neighborhood bully, the neighborhood sissy, and the neighborhood bad boy who becomes the minister. The years pass you see the same type of people in politics, business, medicine and religion. Perhaps a different face, a different name, but it is the same person.

Understanding how these people think and react to certain thoughts and feelings help maximize positive results for you as well as them. Impressions, memories and reactions are like a tapestry. For example when I was four years old my uncle dated two nurses. I became a ploy for him between the two. One nurse brought me to my first movie and swimming for the first time. The other nurse, whom he married, brought me to her hospital and kept showing me around to her friends.

The nurses, with their blue capes, white uniforms with white caps, were to me breathtaking. Becoming a teenager, I gravitated to this look and psyche feel that had developed as a child. This magnetism created compelling forces within me. My parish priest and pastor, Fr. Shrader said, "Can't wait to do your eulogy—you can make people do what they really want to do, but never thought they would or could. No such thing as should, could, impossible—you make it a reality! What God has given you is an awareness to do more with it than anyone else I have known—you take every opportunity to make the most of it." Reflecting back to the 60s, realizing that I could have sunk into depth of an emotional abyss that could have been devastating financially, psychologically to others in my life as well as to myself that might never have gotten back on the course. The best therapy for most problems (blood pressure, arthritis, cancer, cardiovascular problems) and its prevention are the ocean's smell, sound of music, beautiful sights and the human touch. It is intriguing to delve into your inner-self, understanding and seeing who you are as a person. I recall the times at eight or nine years old, the teacher frequently calling on me in class to answer a certain question on the lesson at hand whether it be history, geography, arithmetic or reading a passage in English. The teacher called on me, thinking I was daydreaming because I was looking out the window. In her eyes I was not paying attention to what was being said. Responding with the correct answer would upset her because how could I be daydreaming and be conscious of what she was saying at the same time.

I was extremely shy and until this day am unable to swim because of my reluctance, as a small child, to completely disrobe, a mandatory practice at the local YMCA for boy's swimming class. Continuing this in high school I was shy to disrobe in front of my classmates after the athletic endeavors. It took a few years out of high school and in college before I was comfortable asking a girl out. The first girl I ever asked to go steady was when I was 20, she accepted and we were married two years later.

My life seemingly took on a more aggressive style becoming more extroverted in my overtures toward people in general. I entered the life insurance business in mid 1956, in the field of selling, which was, in many ways, out-of-character for one so painfully shy.

My interest in psychology, philosophy and things of the mind seemed to accelerate in a phenomenal way. In the pursuit of life and all of its bounty, indiscretion and poor judgment intervened. I pursued a relationship with another woman who bore four children out-of-wedlock during the next decade. During this same period five children were born within my marriage. The anguish, the burden, the emotional and the attack of the psyche inflicted by this had its own strange toll on each of the people involved. Ironically, two of the nine children are stronger mentally than if it had never happened. Two of them, I feel, had personal problems in their relationships with the other sex. The two youngest, one is from each side of this relationship, are trying to find themselves. Now that they have married and have beautiful children the missing link is filled. Another son, the oldest, is more his own entity and hopefully at peace with himself. Two children are deceased.

I feel that the woman I vigorously pursued, mother of four of my children, has found peace with me and with herself and, I pray, will be happy and made whole again for the rest of her life. Somehow the connection between my wife and myself is stronger, more loving and bountiful than it ever was or maybe could have been if these happenings had never occurred. The dichotomies to a lesser and greater degree, I understand better are in us all. These paradoxes manifest themselves in different ways whether it be spiritual, materialistic, political, selfishness-unselfishness, love, hate or indifference. Use the positive attributes of our selves in a positive way and use negatives to bring positive results. Life is a mathematical equation. A problem is a chance for growth like a vaccination; it consists of particles of the disease to prevent the disease.

William Shakespeare said four centuries ago, there is humor in tragedy and tragedy in humor. Looking back I see humor in what some would call a tragic circumstance—to have nine offspring between two different mothers in two different homes and being the manager of one company while the leading salesman of another company tires me to recall. In addition, worked out at the athletic club two to three hours every day and socialized with my friends in the evening, it all seems like a dream, with all the confusion, but to me a normal state of affairs with energy and intellect focused while always pursuing my life's work.

Rudyard Kipling's line in the poem, *IF:* If we can meet triumph and disaster and treat those two imposters just the same. I know now thru my life's experiences that the statement the worst that can happen to you might be the best that can happen to you if you don't let it get the best of you-

No one can do two things or be in two places at once and achieve the maximum and the best results for their efforts. This is a fundamental teaching of Zen Buddhism. In the early part of 1960 I was told by Rohrer and Hibler, a mid western psychology group, on an interview study—written and oral—that not anyone had scored the way I had. The psychologist told me that he observed many contradictions in my mental makeup, a dreamer with acute insight, disarming in my philosophical feeling for one so young who had no professional training or education in this area—much intuition—he said.

Buckminster Fuller defines intuition as speeded up intellect. Thinking back to my childhood, my mother would mention, on many occasions, that she talked to so-and-so on the street but she couldn't remember their name. Asking what color were their eyes it was the way that she would say brown, blue or hazel that I could create an image of the person and know who they were. It is known that there are more colors of blue, brown and hazel, due to pigment and shape of eye. The paradoxes of life and living continued on through adolescence into my adulthood.

On entering the insurance business, after leaving school at age 21, I failed the sales aptitude test and the company was not willing to finance me. However, the general agent financed me on the whim of taking a chance on a 20-to-1 shot. The bet paid off for us both. The shyness, the age, the lack of sales and social skills and the fact that I was single is why the company took its position.

The psychological testing five years later was a paradox in form. I joined another insurance group and underwent a battery of tests mentioning to them the Rohrer and Hilber testing, of which they were familiar. However, almost a year later to the day, the psychologist who had interviewed a person in the Norfolk area who was the youngest member of the Million Dollar Round Table and the youngest general agent in the country, wondered whatever had happened to him. He was talking about me to me. I told him ten years later at a cocktail party that I was the same person. Ironically those two occasions ten years before were marked at the same day, same month as the year previous. We also went to the same restaurant, sat at the same table and ordered the same dinner as the year before.

One could say that these were coincidences or accidents, but the dual lifestyle in business and life situations, either consciously or unconsciously, continued for the next twenty years. Even today, subtle overtones are reflected in my business and personal identity. However the source of my independent thinking runs most often against the grain of accepted conventional economic, legal and medical dogma. This is tempered with well thought out economic, legal and medical approaches that are not in acceptance in western thinking. Interesting forces and experiences are being brought forward as we move forward in the 21st century to affirm this way of thought. Albert Schweitzer once said the opposite to courage is not cowardice, but conformity. Many people lead lives of quiet desperation and are more at marking time than living. To be a good example and being your own person is what will make you whole.

Part V:
Essence of Life's Journey and Its Insights

Introspection and Other Observations

The first twenty-five years of my working life I was running in the fast lane—nine children, living by the seat of my pants, taking every dollar to keep my head above water—not knowing whether I would be alive the next year. Selling insurance, drinking, driving, playing basketball, tennis and "kidnapping" people for my weekly soirees seemed to occupy my waking hours. Going to jail, losing my father, mother and son in the early 1980s began to wake me up.

The past twenty years have been of a lower profile enabling me to read more, travel more and move out of a self-destructive path. By decreasing the tempo, I have been able to watch and smell the roses.

The great regret I have had in my life is not spending more quality time with my children. As I write these thoughts, July 20, 1997, feeling this loss for the first time in my life, it is mentally painful. The intense hurt I caused my wife and others by my eschewed judgment and my indiscretions is an indelible mark on my mind. Had the shoe been on the other foot, I don't feel I would have been able to withstand the pain.

It seems that in the order of things I hurt myself the most. When you always are surging forward, throwing caution to the wind, living where angels fear to tread you ask for trouble. I certainly observed this from playing sports, driving a car and living my life. The unfortunate result of this behavior is that it touches on the people you love. The fortunate result of this behavior is that you wake up in time to be aware of your actions and the consequences they can cause for now and generations to follow. Every once in a while one gets a chance to look back into past living and correct itself while there is still the energy and the desire to do so. Over the years we have the chance to meet a plethora of people: different intelligence, backgrounds, outlooks, personalities and character make-ups that form the human being's essence:

It is said that until you walk in another man's shoes, you still are missing a poignant slice of life. This is described in Aristotle's *Rhetoric: Ethos—Pathos—Logos*. To understand empathy, it takes a keen understanding of how a person feels when certain factors come into one's life. Keeping in mind what is logical to one often is illogical to another. Pathos, or emotion, is the third dimension of our triad, many facets trigger love, sadness, greed, fear and joy. We all are unique in our makeup, so there is no constant in the mix of these emotional factors.

July 24, 1997 visiting a well-known psychic, not sure what motivated me to do so, perhaps it was a warning from God, through a medium, to alter my lifestyle or die within five years. Paying attention to who I am, say and do—I am a living example for others.

Noticing as some people age into their 60s, 70s, 80s, their passion is often suppressed by physical handicaps and mental atrophy, their short term memories fade and their perceptions become an overreaction. Events and conversations that at one time were a small piece of the big picture are now isolated due their lack of stimulation.

Science in the decades to come will show that some of the perils of human existence for many are the catalyst for others, better health physically and mentally. Alcohol has certainly been a catalyst for many a person's fall, however in some people it is useful tonic for one's physical and mental health and gives one a potion for keener insights into their own psyche as well other and is capable of life extension. Substance abuse that was an obvious downfall for Keats, Poe and Burns, however was a catalyst for their writing and thinking. Conversely, in the life of probably the world's greatest statesman, Sir Winston

Churchill, it became ironically an asset, probably adding to his greatness and to his longevity. As he once was heard to say, "I have taken more out of alcohol than alcohol has taken out of me." It is of utmost importance to know what is and what is not. The mind must perceive this first to be true and the body has to be in the relevant connection with the mind and its spirit. This thought is certainly looked upon as one of upside down thinking, however gives credence to the axiom "one man's meat is another man's poison."

We are so significant, yet so insignificant, in the grandiose plan of living and dying. Working daily throughout our lives enables us, no matter what our task, to stay in the loop—not to be on the sidelines watching others. Work and life connects itself more by doing than watching.

In Conrad's *Analogy To Reach* this is mentally healthy and adds to our being alive. Why are we seemingly connected in some way to some people and not to others? We cannot explain the subtle nuances that magnetize or pull us back from certain people. Many times these vibes are disingenuous as they are woven into intricate meaning that is beyond most learned and soul-searching men.

There are certain comments that we can make to another with the scenario being the same, deeply affecting one's psyche and to another it has no impact. Seventy-five years ago, when my mother was a young college student, her mother died. On the day of the funeral a lady was overheard saying, "This would be a good home to get into." Later she married my grandfather. Her comments were never forgotten by my mother and her sisters. This could have been an innocent comment or one deeply steeped in ulterior motive. The schism borne out of this comment between stepmother and children altered the family situation and people relationships passing down to generations to come. Introspection is born out of empathy and is a giant step toward making our present and future more fulfilled.

In Ernest Hemingway's classic book, *The Old Man and the Sea*, being in the deep limitless ocean span, alone with your thoughts and the fish below, is poetic beauty of the universe to meet challenges of nature and self: insights—a beauty itself in its mysterious thought. Only people who have things to look forward to are living a full life. Others who have only memories live a shallow existence.

Properly understood, a legend says that the person to whom only memories are left approaches the inorganic state, becoming like stone. Young people have an eager appetite for mental nourishment, especially for what is new. When we get old the appetite in this respect diminishes our thinking. We are unable to swallow and digest all the new thoughts that are served and can take only small bites. We are afraid to bite off more than we can chew. As long as you are young you have many vivid impressions and you welcome and absorb them quickly—when you get old you are less and less impressed and less impressionable. Compassion comes to mind—first the door of your mind is wide open and everybody and everything arriving is welcome. Later that door is only half open and still later it is only just ajar, until finally it is shut—not with a bang, but soundlessly. There is an old song that goes, "Oh Death where is your sting?—I don't care. I have seen everything. Keep young and beautiful if you want to be loved."

George Bernard Shaw, who reached the age of 94, once remarked that old men are dangerous because they have no future as they cannot formulate their thoughts and have not them. They teach all convention with contempt and they can say terrible and terrifying things.

Part VI:
Thinking and Living A Fuller Life

Disraeli, the English philosopher wrote, "Life is too short to be little." Mother Teresa said in Calcutta that India was the second poorest nation on earth—second to the USA—due to moral bankruptcy and thirst for consumerism. The strongest chain, whether a nation or an individual, is only as strong as its weakest link.

We are born and we die. What happens in between is interesting, dream-like, challenging, painful, joyful and an opportunity to multiply ourselves by the thoughts we think and the actions we take. Having the chance to experience pain, pleasure, sorrow, happiness helps us to be more of a person. A stimulus of peak experiences we have had, are having and will have is magnified: our sense of smell, sight, hearing and feeling is heightened in quantum leaps. The panoramic world we are experiencing slowly, however quickly passes. It is our mission to be aware that we savor every minute for our self-fulfilled being. It is our duty to teach our children and theirs, by our example, what we have learned so that we can pass this mantle to the next generation, thereby making life and living a richer and a more complete experience as our Maker intended.

We are creatures of habits—if we don't form good ones we automatically form bad ones. The almost obsessive compulsion that I have found has served me well—that of taking care of things that need to be done and doing them quickly and efficiently gives me an almost ecstatic feeling and gives recreational activities more meaning. Imaging Alexander the Great at age 33, on the steps of the Parthenon, crying, where he had no more worlds to conquer, I can empathize with his mind and his soul.

It is intriguing, how we all are so advanced in some areas and so retarded in other areas. Sitting here in front of a computer screen watching the screen saver with periodic motion of objects in space, realizing how my fingers never have been on a computer keyboard. The computer keyboard in my mind constantly is working and thinking with my imagination in full stride giving meaning to my conceptual thought process of daily living and maximizing interaction with self and others—and not limited by programmed analysis and results. An interesting paradox!

Man is the most fascinating breathing machinery on earth that possesses a soul and is capable of so much greatness and good, while at the same time such bad and evil. We all are motivated by example. Staying in the loop of your work is mentally healthy—as staying in the middle (eye) of the hurricane is safest. Moving toward the problem is to solve—moving away is where the problem gets larger—a perfect mathematical equation. It is important to find the eye of your own hurricane. Life does not pay in counterfeit—if we do more we have more. This has not changed because it is the 21st century.

There is adulation and there is idolatry—adulation being respect and idolatry, taking yourself too seriously. When I think of the British Empire and its fantasy world—king, queen, prince and princess—I think of the fairy tale world. The blueblood syndrome gives an exaggerated pomp and circumstance in the monarchy as well as many of the rank and file and it's myth. This creation dilutes the reality of living. We see in our own nation the protocol, the black robe of the judicial system becomes more of a humorous anecdote in its trials and trial by one's peers is more humorous than being equitable and honest.

May you live in interesting times is an old Chinese curse meaning that life has to be somewhat in turmoil to be exciting, challenging and interesting. Thriving on this thinking keeps our mind, wits alive and our endorphins flowing to help us to live more fully (the safest place to be is in the eye of the storm). Living in peace with oneself and speaking succinctly, however quietly, we are heard and better understood. To be respected is to respect, to be loved is to love, and to be understood is to understand. The fact that still waters run deep is not only for the lakes and oceans, but for man as well. An ounce of words is a pound of thought. Thoreau once said we are richer for the things we can do without.

Often when we feel so smart we are beginning to get dumb. Understanding the dynamics of people, intelligence and beauty, ugliness, good and bad, love, hate can fulfill and give meaning in most every facet of our lives and help explain the paradoxes that are present in us. The old axiom of centuries ago: when we are green we begin to grow, when we think we are ripe we begin to rotten hasn't changed because we are entering the 21st century. It is a continuing odyssey to see how people react to life's happenings. There are one-man women and one-woman men—meaning that these people are so structured, either by religious belief or inherent qualities by heredity, they cannot and will not, in most instances, ever be with another, regardless of their spouses removal from the scene by divorce, death or separations.

The words "addict/aholic", whether it is one who uses alcohol, gambling, smoking, working, religious, political, usually denotes less than favorable thoughts. However, in every walk of life there are places for zealot leaders and those who are focused in accomplishing certain ends. People, more often than not, are contradictions in their thinking and doing. Knowing who we are and keeping the mind clear is of utmost importance in reaching the goals we have set for ourselves, whether it is our health or material gain. If we can reflect upon the deep insights from our childhood experiences and associations as well as memories of our feeling and thinking in years gone by, it will give you a stronger grip on events happening to you. By pursuing this course we literally can taste the sweetness and richness of being and all of its fruit. To learn that these childhood reactions and attitudes transcend into our attitudes in our experiences as we become adults. We are as happy as we make up our mind to be—the mind is the pilot of our life—it is everything—our soul, spirit and essence.

Let's look at timing at another place in time:

1943—during the Nazi rein over Europe in the holocaust—Auschwitz—for every man caught trying to escape, ten men were killed. One man sobbed asking what would become of his family—another man stepped forward and offered himself in the other man's place and then faced the firing squad, allowing the other man to live. It is realized that he was dedicated to the Virgin Mary, always referring to her as The Immaculate. He initiated universities, did much good and after his death was canonized as St. Maximillion. However, it is known that thousands of men have given their lives to save others in the wars since the beginning of time after living lives of wonderful example. Their personal courage and feats are, most times, unknown and their lives, particularly in wars of exercise, go unrecognized and they die, seemingly in vain.

Timing again identifies itself, undeniably important connection in the outcome of life situation and life pursuits and often in death and life happening. There is no question that some humans are star-crossed as true as others have a certain aura that follows them about their daily going and coming. Playing and working daily throughout our lives enables us, no matter what our task, to stay in the loop—not to be on the sidelines watching others do their daily task.

Truth is what you are meant to be. The love of self is so important (not a narcisstic love), but a love that is contagious, pure and giving.

Three friends, all of whom are over 80, I have observed a similar thread running through each: passion. Interesting thoughts make the happiest people, those with a wisdom borne out of their experiences and interactions with others. When you can talk to a person for six to eight hours at a time there is a magnetic force present, they as yourself become a bigger and richer human being. On the other end of the age spectrum, there are three 35 year and younger friends makeup part of my life board of directors. They are gifted with brains, ambition, excitement and that important word—PASSION. One of these is my son. In each case these human beings draw big circles. Their minds are like sponges and their endurance is unequalled. They have and are becoming more of a person each moment they live.

There are investments, playing tennis and basketball for example, that have been for fun, never exercising for health. My board of directors has been my conduit for growth—which is my passion.

Pursuing with a sense of fascination and curiosity the patina look in homes, cars, clothes and having self-awareness for health maintenance, a God-given luck that didn't require me to sacrifice because it already is in my orientation. Striving to be all we can be is what is important memories of years ago are how we arrive to the present. It was once said that our parents decided before we were born who we were going to be—genes, environment, only who we will become is the X factor.

The father of medicine, Sir William Osler, says that we all live in day tight time compartments—when we reach out and feel more we are more and living is so much sweeter. We must love ourselves to love another—we are a reflection of what we read and think.

My son, Tim, had a host of physical and mental problems. When he died, his older sister commented, "I don't think he ever had the experience of being with a woman." However, he became, in some areas, a fulfilled human being, more alive than you or me through his handicaps and his unconditional love of people.

Yesterday I talked to my cousin. The two of us have talked no more than half a dozen times in the last 50 years. As I reflect on our conversation this Sunday afternoon, I realized that although he is just two years younger, his single life and habits of being in bed by 8:00 PM and up by 3:00 AM is almost diametrically opposite to my life style. His arriving at his office at 7:30 AM daily and home by 4:30 PM only avails himself of less than four daylight hours.

Today, two weeks to the day, I received a call from another cousin who lives within a few miles of the one with whom I talked two weeks ago, telling me that our cousin, Mike, died in his sleep this morning.

Mike lived by himself for himself, which ironically kept him from fulfilling himself as a person.

Reflecting again on our words of a fortnight ago, I realize that if he had had a soul mate and was fortunate to have extension of himself he would, in my mind, still be alive today. Social networking has been proven to prolong living and add to the quality of life itself. That is why our bonding with others is a healthy and priceless investment. Monetarily speaking, his pension from the government vanished with his last breath. That would have been worth over two million dollars over normal life expectancy. This shows how relative and temporary most things are—including life here on earth.

Affectively knowing this after all these years, it is time to think in using my mind to protect my well-being: physically, mentally and spiritually as time is fleeting. Yesterday I had the first full blood work, or any blood-work except what was required when Anne and I were married in February 1957. I am sure that the psychic's message, intuitive feeling and the death of my blood cousin—all occurring within the last week, precipitated this. Fortunately the blood work was the best that the physician had ever seen with low (130/80) blood pressure, a total of 150 cholesterol and good chemistry. My life has been, in many ways an abuse of my temple, however, ironically, its abuse became a plus in my life. I have been accused many times during the course of my life of being a walking dichotomy, which have transcended into my very blood makeup—a collector's item if you will.

A self-surrender—that existence is meaningful, that my life had a goal. Antoine Saint-Expurey has defined love as the process of my leading you back to yourself. He suggests that a growing self brings with it a growing love. You have no choice but to love for when one does not he finds his alternatives lie in destruction and despair. With each person who suffers we too suffer a little. We exist for each individual as each individual exists for us all.

The perfect love would be one that gives all and expects nothing—unconditional love. One loves because he wills it, because it gives him joy—he knows that growth and discovery of oneself depends upon it. Buddha said, "You are on the way to enlightenment when you cease desiring."

Think of what men have said in their songs: *Love is a Many Splendored Thing; What the World Needs Now is Love Sweet Love; Love is what makes the world go 'round.* Love is the answer; You're Just in Love—When my heart goes pitter-patter and skips a beat. Looking back—family, friend, and childhood mates—these are life's pearls.

As Christ said, "No greater love hath any man than to lay down his life for his fellow man. Love is the finest tonic for health, happiness and filling the unforgiving minute. Giving is the only time that you have true power.

We cognitively know time is passing, when we know it affectively we really know it. When we relate to what we were doing 20 years ago, 10 years, it seems like it took forever to go from 1 to 10/10 to 20/20 to 30/but then it accelerated. We must increase our awareness to grow as humans—to be happy, fulfilled and to be at peace with ourselves, become more of a person as shown in Victor Frankl's book, *Man's Search for Meaning*. We all draw circles—some large, some small—however the larger the circle the greater the experience. We only live at 5% capacity; the problem is conformity; which is a form of cowardice. Einstein's statement that imagination is supreme to knowledge, by getting in touch with yourself, you get in touch with your essence—your intuition, your will, your love, your compassion and strength.

To know how to separate the wheat from the chaff is the value of an education. Value of judgment is usually wrong. Gut feeling lends to Easy—Energetic—Effortless, being my guide. Finding true conversation is an interpretation of hearing a genuine intercourse of souls, to touch matter that concerns the soul.

Cicero, a first century BC Roman orator, said you know a person best when you know the driving spirit that shapes his life. These are facets of the soul: fears, passion, longings, memories, and emotion.

Part VII:
Dynamics of Life's Investments

That beautiful feeling that transpires between father and son, teacher and student, mother and daughter, husband and wife, is a wonderful show of giving where one gives to another and the getting comes back to the giver by fulfilling the hopes and dreams of both. What we do in life is an investment: the people we have known, the places we have been, the flowers we have smelled, the music we have heard, the things we have seen with our own eyes. The things we know because of this is one of God's special treats to us—so that we may enjoy and something to pass on to others as they cross our path and come into our lives. The investment in ratio to time and length of investment has been my wife and secondly my children. Every moment and every day is a phenomenal wonder and an investment so unique we must learn from it, as it will not be repeated ever again in the same way we experienced it.

When I married "my own true love" which happened to be our song shortly after our meeting in the winter of 1955, we were both virgins and maintained our celibacy until the day we married February 9, 1957. The marriage, I believe, was made in heaven. Feeling that way then and feel that way now.

Fate has strange twists and turns because in the late part of the year 1958 I met a nurse at the local Naval Hospital. A relationship developed and continued for the next 21 years, producing four children, who I financially supported, maintaining two separate residences in the same city. The children have the same surname as my wife and the five children we had in our marriage, two of whom are deceased.

Feeling the dynamics of this relationship was of such a blend of psyches that had any of the three adults been changed in the least iota, the relationship would have disintegrated in the first few years. On reflecting on what spurred the bonds of the relationship there was a certain belief that things would be resolved and life would become less tangled. All parties are monogamous in their thinking and compassionate in their feelings. Being loyal to their beliefs there was a certain innocence that prevailed as found in a young child. This dual relationship came to an end in the fall of 1979. My wife and I still live in the same city as before and are happily married.

Reflecting back over the years, the first seven years from originally meeting the nurse, that relationship began to deteriorate due to lack of solid foundation of family, friends and not having the comfort and peace and security that bonds man and woman together.

We all are responsible for our own lives, that believing in another and following their heart can be, has been and always will be a path filled with pitfalls. One's greatest asset like devotion, compassion can become one's liability.

The relationship with my children, conceived outside of marriage, is quite strong with one child and almost acquaintance-like with the other three. The relationship with my wife ironically has strengthened a thousand fold because by some turn of fate this three-way relationship happened. My three surviving children with my wife, the bonding is good with two and moderate with the youngest one.

I hope that as time passes the relationships with all my offspring will strengthen and grow. When I get into my own psyche and analyze the whys and hows of my life I can get an insight into some of my actions. For example, going back to when I was four or five years old, it is as if it were yesterday, my uncle was dating two nurses: one in the Navy at that same hospital referred to earlier and the other at a local civilian hospital in the small town of Portsmouth, VA. These two nurses with their white uniforms and blue capes fascinated me, being upset, when he married. I was six years old; she was my first love and this strong emotional feeling transcended into my adult life with the nurse I was aligned for two decades.

When we are young we all have these active imaginations that take us into many realms of thinking. I remember at 10 or 11 years old organizing a team of where I was captain and star quarterback making up stories of how we played this team and that team and give a play-by-play description to some of my young friends of a team and game that didn't exist. This was imagination—a wondrous example of the make-believe life.

When I was in my mid 20s my business was mostly with doctors—so much that time I would take over this imaginary role for playful enjoyment of other people's minds.

In my late 30s and early 40s, I drove a car without a license due to traffic infractions by the dozens. I drove with two different drivers' licenses, neither being mine. I was incarcerated for about a year for this habitual offender status after attending two different Alcohol Safety Action programs simultaneously. In both situations the drivers' license, I possessed in names other than my own.

Looking back in these scenarios it was all imagination, make-believe and an excitement of living on the edge. Please don't throw me in the briar patch, but that's where I really wanted to be. Remember comfort is staying in the eye of the hurricane. We must all know our limitations, which keeps us sane. The mind is the master weaver both of the inner garment and the outer garment of circumstance. That as they have woven in ignorance and pain they may now weave in enlightenment and happiness. As a man thinketh in his heart so is he! When we see people we don't like we are seeing ourselves—we are all mirrors. Listen to what one doesn't say and if you pay close attention it will tell you more than what he did say.

I believe in living deliberately and interestingly so that when death comes one will not discover that he had not lived. Even the expression on our face affects the way our blood flows, our inner peace. The endorphins transcend our very being. Expanding human awareness is something we should always be pursuing and we will then draw big circles and broaden our insight and the depth of our being. When we love another he or she becomes my mirror and I become his or hers. Being there is essential to our self-worth. Thriving on this keeps our wits about us and our endorphins flowing to lead fuller lives—to be more of a person.

James Joyce, in his masterpiece, *Ulysses*, ends the book with the greatest affirmation in literature where he has Molly sigh over several pages, "Yes, yes, yes, oh yes, yes, yes!!!!!" That beautiful feeling that transpires between father and son, teacher and student, mother and daughter, husband and wife, is a wonderful show of giving where one gives to another and the getting comes back to the giver by the givee by fulfilling the hopes and dreams of them both. We soon become part of which we have known, have been, and feel.

When we help others we help ourselves more often in a much more holistic way, physically, mentally, and spiritually. We all have contradictions in our make-up as we know love and hate are closely aligned; genius and idiocy. Beauty and ugliness interface—we can see beauty and ugliness in all we see before us if we look deeply enough,

As in Charles Dickens' *Tale of Two Cities,* "It was the best of times, it was the worst of times. It was the age of wisdom and it was the age of foolishness. It was the path of belief; it was the epoch of incredulity. It was the season of darkness; it was the spring of hope. It was the winter of despair. We had nothing before us. We were all going directly to heaven or we all were going directly the other way. These are the times that try men's souls". These words written 140 years ago confirm that men don't change, but times do.

We must all gravitate to the positive use of food, exercise, fluids and foods and to understand and stay away from the things that become our nemesis. Only those who see the invisible can do the impossible as this applies to our human frailties and our interactions with others as well as the world.

Part VII: Dynamics of Life's Investments 41

Mindless motions and thinking in neutral does not allow one to go forward with their intentions and buried thoughts don't surface but remain buried. We must adhere to our gut feelings in who we are and how we think and to learn by example and cultivating our minds to bring us to where we want to be.

Looks, smells and feels bring back fond memories of days gone by and allow us to smooth our ride into the future. The sayings "have a nice day", "how are you doing?" are reactionary moves—not thinking. The interactions for the betterment of ourselves and who we direct them to by imaging what we are saying and letting it penetrate both the greeter and the greeted who are enhanced by its richness. Reflection is brought forth as everyone brings out different facets of our makeup and to understand and learn how they shape us makes life a more interesting and enjoyable adventure.

When I was in my mid 20s to early 40s I spent an unnecessary sum of monies on expensive cars: Jaguars, Cadillacs and spent an inordinate amount of monies in bars and clubs. Now a firm advocate of older expensive, larger, well-kept other people's cars as my transportation mode in such a way that I wouldn't trade my low priced '86 Town Car with 250,000 miles for a new Lexus or BMW even—except to trade for its redeeming value. The cost of high insurance, maintenance and taxes are eliminated.

Real living and thinking has more substance, meaning and appreciation. By paying attention and having passion for reading, traveling, thinking and life with friends and family, life becomes more beautiful. Hopefully, by setting example, on condemnation of waste, mindlessness and life pursuits that are harmful, artificial and lean toward style rather than substance a better person, a better way of life evolves.

There will be a time like a new world opening up that I can say to my daughter, Mary, whom I honestly love and she will say I honestly love you. The day will come because I see it in my mind's eye. I know this will come to be with sons Patrick, John and Richard. Being able to see it and feel it with my whole being and when that day comes we all will come back whole. Son, Michael, and daughters, Elizabeth and Kristina, are on board and are as beautiful as the day they were born. I would like now to express to the starship of my life the thoughts on my wife, Anne. My feelings for her run much deeper than sometimes I realize. She is the most caring, loving, dedicated human that I have ever known. My mother used to say many years ago "Anne can keep up with you." I knew then as I know now how true this is. I have always admired her inner beauty that is made that way by her innocence, honesty, intelligence as well as her dry sense of humor that seems to spirit many conversations and experiences. I often chide her about her innocence and her patronizing of others. Her comment to this rings true as she says that it is good for me that she does patronize, because of the trying times we have been through, she would not still be there. It is interesting the dynamics of rich feelings and unconventional love that transcends our bonding. Our dissimilarities are ironically our strengths. I am awed how she challenges me mentally and probes to make more of myself, encouraging and inspiring and looking for what is good, healthful and enjoyable for me. Know that she feels often that I would rather be with my friends going here and there, however there is nobody that I enjoy being with more than Anne, thinking, loving, philosophizing and sharing my innermost feelings. I have never known before anybody who has the strength of spirit and character that is hers alone. Whether it is my Irish luck or my destiny, I am a better human being by having her come into my life and am simply, when all is said and done, the luckiest person on the face of the earth.

As we are all mirrors, I was fortunate that my mother and father "got together." To be born of good genes and given the breath of life by Almighty God, the greatest gift that anyone can have. In many ways living a charmed life in spite of myself—beautiful wife, children, friends and places been and things I know, have seen and heard are breathtaking. I am a passionate person who loves life and what it has to offer more than anyone I have ever known. There have been masses of contradictions that I initially became aware of in my teenage years that have carried through my life, paradoxically have served me well in my business and my personal life. Realizing that having the proper chemistry with another, as with my wife, is an essential mandatory facet in my life's situations so we can both be all that we can be. The synergetics is fascinating. Being proud of my Irish background, I am aware that it is what gives me passion, energy, steadfastness, as well as an uncanny insight into other people's thinking and feeling. Enjoying somewhat of being a rebellious person, always thinking, feeling and liking people who are true to themselves and live with a purpose. Having gargantuan appetites in almost every phase of my existence: learning, working, drinking, living and always seeking and reaching. I live in the eye of the hurricane, I have enjoyed being thrown in to the "briar patch"; it is a challenge to survive and feel the adrenalin flow as well as the psychic income pour forth. Constantly curious and fascinated by what tomorrow brings. Knowing full well that example is the most powerful motivation that there is. Feeling sometimes that I can be a wonderful example. I try to be "ready for anything", knowing I have chameleonic abilities.

Anne, my Sunshine, I love you for drawing out of me all the beautiful things no one else had looked hard enough to find.

Part VIII:
Life's Challenge—Dyadics of Relationships

"Gentlemen, start your engines!" My son Michael while in Rome, Italy with his mother recently voiced this comment. They had met with Cardinal Pio Laghi at the Vatican, who recommended that they visit the Nervi auditorium. On inquiry to the Swiss Guard regarding admittance, the guard replied "impossible." Mike's response was, "Does that sound like gentlemen, start your engines?" They proceeded to the auditorium, presented Mike's letter of introduction to the Cardinal from the Ambassador of American States and were admitted. I know the challenge came to him honestly.

Reflecting back to when my playmates said I couldn't do this or that something deep inside me compelled me to prove them wrong. As a junior in high school the basketball coach benched me due to a constant static between myself and one of the other players whose twin was the star player. Telling the coach that I would get four players from off the street and beat his team, he laughed saying that we didn't have a chance. The dare was taken and did indeed defeat my high school team with me being the leading scorer (they were the Virginia state champions that year).

On entering the life insurance business after leaving college I was told that I couldn't sell, based on the company's sales aptitude test. On a hunch the manager hired me and I became the youngest member of the Million Dollar Round Table. The manager told me that the aptitude test was like assessing the odds on a favorite in a horse race, however the one thing that was hard to detect was the desire of the horse.

Entering the Army by way of the draft, I deliberately did not pass the mental test. Then as now this would have been a waste of time, money and thinking. The nation's problems are beset with much waste in these areas. After 30 days I was discharged to continue my life's pursuits. Ironically, the manager's hiring me in spite of my not passing the aptitude test for sale of life insurance presented an interesting paradox. My trainer told me if I didn't stop selling life insurance as an investment I would not succeed. After 45 years—he didn't last in the business and I did. Insurance is an excellent piece of property.

Due to this hell bent thinking of the challenge of the moment reared itself in many ways. As time passed, most situations were served well over the years by having this tenacious I CAN DO approach to life. When one has to be creative it is intriguing how the mind can be as thinking evolves.

Desperate times demand desperate measures. The mental adrenaline comes forth, which meets the present challenge. Finding in personal as well as business involvements ways to keep the mind razor sharp. The cliché of when we stop teaching we stop learning is vital to understand. The mouse in the corner with the cat in pursuit is experiencing a feeling of accelerated instincts to survive that it would be unable to feel under normal conditions. The human instincts are on a higher level when threatened by fire, gunshot, drowning, or losing his balance in a high place. The importance of calm reaction and rational thinking diminishes the harm that can occur.

Living, I feel, is a vibrant state of being. We know we have felt, seen and heard others who are alive literally, but not really. There is no excitement in their eyes, their voices or their bodies a sense of suspension. They are breathing and just existing. The endorphins have diminished, their bodies are atrophied as well as their mind, their spirit is nonexistent and living borders on passionless.

It is fascinating to remember certain thoughts people have voiced that are insightful. Most often remembering only one comment or situation that stands out in my mind of all their words and thoughts. A friend made the comment, "Our bodies are just transports of our brains," this being said on a cool Saturday in spring, during the month of April, at approximately 2:00 PM. These observations have been there since I was a child.

Years ago an acquaintance of ours made a passing observation that my wife and I needed to take care of each other. The thought becomes more ingrained in our actions toward each other as time goes by. It is thoughts like these that, if heeded, can increase our quality of living and give more strength to the "pay attention" syndrome. Many times on entering a room I can feel the electricity or the lack of it coming from the people there. These electrical charges are essential in our dynamics with others.

Penning these thoughts a few days before my youngest son's wedding, October 10, 1998, which by chance is the anniversary of my mother and father's wedding October 10, 1933. Every situation and event has a unique tapestry woven into it. My youngest son's wedding, as well as my oldest daughter's wedding, I was not invited, nor to their high school or college graduations. This stems from another October 10, 1958 when I met their mother and subsequently four children were born. Marriage never followed the sequence of these events and over the years the dynamics of family relationships were, then and now, forever altered with contradictory feelings permeating the thought of this current generation and their spouses and the new generation of grandchildren—neither knowing the real feelings of the people and how it affects their psyche.

The time since the beginning of my marriage and having five children that paralleled my other life which stopped after two decades, gave me the stability and roots needed to bypass a dysfunctional flawed lifestyle for a happy, fulfilling life with a wife and children. Life's journey has been a most interesting odyssey and worthy fulfillment of being part of my children's graduations, marriages and grandchildren's adoring love—hopefully God willing, the best is yet to come!

Part VIII: Life's Challenge—Dyadics of Relationships

No sadder words of tongue or pen are those words "what might have been" seems a fitting epilogue to this chapter of life. Author, Gail Sheehy, in her book, *Understanding Man's Passages*, states, "instead of being warrior and provider, men can now become the kind of fathers their own fathers were not. They can become closer to their wives and connect with their feelings and that's better than any magic bullet"

Having the right mate is the key to life. They say that God looks after fools and children, of whom I have been both, and He certainly looked after me, in spite of my Irish rebel ways, and myself by sending me my wife. The challenges of life, marriage and living, met together as husband and wife and enduring the times makes the pact strong and beautiful beyond description.

On a lighter side of thinking, Steinhilber's Restaurant is a point in practice. Being a patron for over 40 years and the only one who can bring brown water into his house, the owner said," If you are with Don its ok—if you are not with him you can't bring the brown water". This happened out of dynamics born out over decades of interpersonal relationship that originated before we were born with his family and my own.

There seems to be a cognitive natural awareness of what to eat and what not to eat or drink, proving that you can outlive most of the clean livers. Drinking can be a catalyst to the intensity of thinking, thanks to your genes.

Sensitivity increases dramatically on the non-drinkers part and brings improper assessment of the physical and mental state of the drinker. This is due to levels of thinking that are subtle and imperceptible in the dynamics of the drinker and the non-drinker—the non-drinker falsely seeing things changing in the thinking of the drinking individual when in fact the drinker is becoming more sensitive and aware of himself.

There is a time when this can change as judgment leaves the imbiber and awareness can become oblivious to outside influences. Sometimes thoughts flow into your head when drinking that are clearer than when not drinking.

The world of doublespeak and double meaning transcend into some interesting paradoxes in perception: The physician who says of the patient who has just died, "Well, I threw everything at her." The attorney becomes a silver tongued devil speaking to exonerate his client or to convict the defendant with the truth be damned. The human chess game continues with the patient, the client, and the voter as mere pawns in the big picture. Life, death, freedom are paid homage, however more often than not they are mere words in life's games. The song of the 50s, written by a black, gay, blind man, Tommy Edwards, *It's All in the Game,* brings forth some of these thoughts. Ironically, if you know how to play the game it has the power to conquer all. All facets of living, thinking and feeling are multi dimensional.

Filling the unforgiving minute gives credence to *waste not—want not.* Divide and multiply in your thoughts and actions you become happier and stronger, spiritually and physically. Welcome sad times and bad times as it makes you more in touch with the happy and good times. Sometimes feeling so good I deliberately subject myself to negative people and situations that will stabilize my temperament.

All we do in life is an investment—every moment in time, every week and every day. The main reason we wouldn't want to live our lives over again is because we have a unique psychic income in the friends we made and the places we have been. Most of us do not realize that staying alive and well has to do mostly with our attitudes. The endorphins running through our bodies make us happier and have healthier minds. To be always excited about life and the passion of living it to the fullest is the medicine says the Lord. It is the way we react to life's situations is what makes us stronger. Handicaps are merely chances for growth.

Having an insight to our childhood memories, our likes and dislikes, the whys of these likes and dislikes, as well as how we related to our parents and our playmates. It gives us a clearer understanding of

Part VIII: Life's Challenge—Dyadics of Relationships 49

how we relate to our wife, children and friends. This enables us to maximize our thinking and the dynamics of our relationships by tapping the potential in our daily lives. Visualizing how interaction with others and events that happened in our life unfolds. We must attempt to see the invisible, if you will, so we can do the impossible and become more alive. Realize how we bond every once in a while, sometimes only once or twice in a lifetime, with another, it is then we can understand the deepest part of our psyche and the motivations from our soul.

The expressions on your face, the way our blood flows, is our inner peace. We should remember that throughout life there is an ebb and flow you should not fight.

The mind is the master weaver, both of the inner garment and the outer garment of circumstance, "as a man thinketh in his heart so is he." When we see people we don't like, often we are seeing ourselves.

To know when to hold them and to know when to fold them, to know when to walk away and to know when to run, is an opening line of Kenny Rogers' song, *The Gambler*, is appropriate in our relationships and maximizes our time on earth. Feeling sometimes in my relationships with people being with them and not with them simultaneously. What they are saying and thinking, is being blessed and cursed with this insight. Knowing that it is better to tell the truth and not lie, cheat or steal. It makes you feel better. There are occasions one cannot afford to tell the truth because of the nature of the person with whom you are speaking.

Observing over my lifetime conversations with certain people are reasons for doing something or not doing something. If you concede to their position when you know they are wrong you are affirming their actions. They will then believe what they are thinking and doing is right. You are doing them a disfavor. This thinking, if left unchecked, has serious consequences in other areas. It is like giving a permission slip to a young child, which shades his reasoning and judgment.

It has been fascinating how one can inject words and thoughts in one's thinking as if it came from another and believe it affirms their position. Liken to the demonstration, to the courtroom antics of prosecutor and defense, eliciting thoughts from the defendant and their vocalizing these thoughts in an entirely different mode than what was said. The media is guilty of this daily in their attempt to communicate what one says and what one does not say. Reminding me of the adage figures don't lie but liars can figure. This happens in the financial world, by way of computers and mathematical interpretations. One is attracted to, for example, the gingerbread in a house, car and people and the essence is overlooked. For example, the color of the car, the radio, becomes the factors to which the individual is attracted. In women it is often their legs, breasts, buttocks, not their mind and heart. One buys a house because of its sauna, swimming pool, and wallpaper, not for its construction or its practicality of living space.

The whole is greater than the sum of its parts, whether it is a human being, a picture or a play. The components fit together in harmony, but often contrast making harmony. The synergy of thinking, feeling and conversing fuels one's energy and imagination to create many times works of art—be it a painting, a building or a successful business transaction. In our interaction with others a certain thought, word or look could change a strained relationship.

As a young child, my mother encouraged me to read *The Art of Thinking* by Ernest Dimnet. I discovered many interesting observations of how one person reacts toward another on the same subject, witnessing an interesting phenomenon that one displays in his daily attitude in responding to another's request or another's thoughts. There are certain people with whom we have a natural and stronger bonding. The ease of one person's thinking flows so naturally and unimpeded to the lucid thinking and good feeling flow between the two.

When we think of our car, home, our friends, these are reflections of who we are and aspire to be in our needs and wants. If we delve into our psyches, we discover by the way we speak, act, think and feel is a composite of why, how and who we are. If we go back to when we were just an infant, we developed a security blanket syndrome that was shown through our attachment to the little play dog or bear that we brought everywhere we went. This transcends in our feeling for certain situations, places and people we find ourselves attracted.

Man is a complicated organism, a walking dichotomy whose strength is his weakness and his weakness his strength. The essence of his being rests on his passion, genes and environment. The cliché that one man's meat is another man's poison relates to his mental and physical immune system and his perception of a situation. For example, let's take the individual who is so conscious of paying too much for an article of clothing, a piece of furniture, food, gas and shoes, is almost removed from watching an investment go down and the proper measures to correct it. The weakness or the habit can be strength in one instance and this same strength works against him in another situation.

I realize that I was fortunate in that my mother and father got together. It was only for the grace of God that I had such wonderful parents and a close-knit family. Family bonding is an important foundation for your thinking in life, seeing me thru trying times in business and personal life making me hang on, whereby, without it, I could have mentally harmed myself and people who were closest to me.

Looking back at my business life, its rewards were many, the freedom that it allowed me to enrich myself in other areas. The people met throughout the country and world would have been virtually impossible without it. Many of these found friendships still exist today and are but another dimension in enlarging the circle of life.

Ironically due to my permissive lifestyle my freedom provided me with adventures as far out as being incarcerated for eight months in the early '80s, for driving automobiles under a revoked driver's permit, to as mild as my social club escapades, from which I was suspended for thirty days. A letter from the president of a local club:

Dear Mr. Foster:

I am sure you understand that it was with a great deal of regret the House Committee was obliged to recommend to the Board of Directors that you be suspended from this Club for a period of thirty days, and that the Board was equally reluctant to order your suspension.

For your information a series of incidents led to the unhappy decision. You were observed to have brought a local resident, who would otherwise be eligible for membership, to The Harbor Club more than four times in a calendar year. You and that particular guest exasperated several members of the House Committee, whom you probably did not recognize at the time, by your gluttonous consumption of complimentary hors-d'oeuvre prepared and served each evening for the membership. On one occasion, you were observed to remove the whole chafing dish of hot hors-d'oeuvre to your table and serve your guests therefrom and on another occasion in the presence of two members of the House Committee, you and your friend consumed fifty-four pieces of cold hors-d'oeuvre. On one occasion you tied up one of the two telephone lines servicing the Club for more than forty-five minutes making business calls, and less than two weeks thereafter, having been requested not to do so, you repeated the performance. Finally, on November 4, having registered for light luncheon service in the lounge area of the Club, you elected to remove a piece of pastry from the desert wagon, consumed enroute to the elevator, and never reported the same for charge to any one of the help.

After a consideration of all of these incidents, each of which was verified, the Board reached the conclusion that your conduct was ungentlemanly, to say the least.

The Board regrets that you did not appear to explain your behavior when given the opportunity to do so.

Sincerely,

Wm. I. Dickson, Jr., President

The episode of eight months confinement was something I wouldn't trade for the experience was interesting and brought into a world that teaches you about people and their lives. I remember a prominent attorney friend of the family saying, "For Don this is just another adventure. His grandchildren are going to have a colorful grandfather".

Now as I put a closure on my business life, my escapades and dedicate the next phase of living to broadening my interest in life, its people and hopefully passing that wisdom to the next generation.

It is almost frightening to be in some of life's situations and understanding people's feelings and thinking, yet to be mentally removed from it. Many times, when you think that you have a problem it is a problem because you think that it is a problem. Conversely, if you look upon the supposed problem as a truly an asset and an opportunity for broadening your circle you then have the solution. Buddhism, for example, shows that pain is pleasure and pleasure is pain. If you grasp the depth and meaning of this you can apply it to the daily challenges we all face.

The rhyme, "One night I saw a man upon the stair. A little man who wasn't there. He wasn't there again today. Oh how I wish he would go away" certainly points out that Pogo's, "We have seen the enemy and it is us".

Personally, some things in your life and business life are not meant to be. It is an exercise to pursue certain people as well as business situations over and over because there is a dynamic that has to be created between you and the subject at hand or your pursuits are in vain. I affectively know the above to be true now. This is a revelation making me appreciate my interaction with others.

Realizing how many experiences I have not had and things I have not done:

Never been in water over my head

Never fished, hunted, or gambled

Never had a doctor, lawyer, accountant or had my fingers on a computer

Never used but one hair tonic, only had one job in my married life

Always had faith, hope and love in others and myself. Always been lucky, mischievous and always had fun. Always had the best of life, children, parents, friends, and feeling. Always been incredibly curious, fascinated by life and all its beauty, wonder and fantasy. Always been my worst enemy, best friend and confidant. Always lived on the edge and loved every minute of it.

The best of times sometimes are the times that spoil you and the worst of times are the times that can give you the most appreciation, insight and know these are the times you can learn the most, feel the deepest and see the futherest. The worst times usually have been a state of mind.

In the draft, for example, mentioned earlier, the advocacy of honor, duty and country is falsely portrayed. The real honor is to serve your God, family and self, and then your country is better served as well. When you become part of the osmosis process you are a liability to all concerned. I was determined not to become part of the waste factor.

Conspicuous consumption hurts all: the giver, the taker and the citizenry because another facet of waste has been put into motion. Who said that one man's trash is another man's treasure brought forth an important lesson that if mankind abided by, would be healthier, happier both physically and mentally.

Part IX:
Times of My Life and Civil Disobedience

Twenty years ago Warner Bros. labeled me a concrete cowboy and I was sentenced to two alcohol safety action programs. Ironically, going through them (each a ten-week course) under two separate names, neither of which was mine—attended these classes back-to-back. It was an interesting and "living on the edge" experience. When my driver's license was returned, it was sent in care of an attorney friend living out of state. The adrenalin present from this experience was another thing that made life invigorating because of the inherent danger.

The day: December 16, 1981. The place: Traffic court—Virginia Beach, Virginia with The Honorable Calvin Spain presiding. The motion driving under the influence continued against Donald Patrick Foster alias Christopher Clark. The identity is requested and motion is granted. Bond is posted and case is continued. Judge Spain gives defendant a $1,000.00 fine and finds him guilty of DUI and sentences him to one year in jail and six months revocation of his license. For the habitual offender charge, bond has been denied by the Honorable John Preston on December 16 and again on January 19 and again by the Honorable Philip Russo on the grounds of "danger to himself and public."

The situation, however, remains no bond—the events of the last forty-five days have been most revealing: The first few days you can't believe it is happening to you. You are incarcerated-the second day in solitary confinement. However, you convince yourself after day one you will get bond, after day two that bond will be issued. After day three you realize that you are going to be in jail for the next ten days thru the Christmas holiday. The days fade into nights and back into days. The weather outside is rainy. The feelings of shock, disbelief, acceptance, hope and fruitless wait go on with the balance of emotions going from disbelief to shock, hope, acceptance, resentment to the whole gamut all over again as in a cancer patient who has been told he is terminally ill.

Your days are planned around waking at 5:30, eating at 6:30, reading to 9 and waiting for lunch at 11:00 with writing letters, thinking, looking out the barred window and wondering when you will be on the other side.

After a few weeks of sleeping upon the floor (not enough beds), you become somewhat institutionalized—listening for the guard's keys, the word "chow", the look out of your cell—waiting for that five minutes on the telephone twice a week and the 20 minute visit from your family. The wait is interminable in the passing of time, as the days turn into weeks and the weeks into months. The time has come where the other seven inmates and yourself must pull as a team to tolerate the long hours of getting thru the days. The 20 minutes at the library once a week, the 10 minutes of phone calls and the 20-minute visit once a week become the ultimate highlight of your week. Sometimes the three meals a day is all that adds interest to your life.

The temperature inside the jail remains constant and the lives drone on. The maximum-security area remains on hold. Sentences range from one year to 100 years.

If hopes become too high for parole, reduction of sentence, hopes are dealt a severe blow psychologically. A balance of objective thinking must be sought to access one's future, its options as well as its impact on our lives.

In retrospect, a more positive rehabilitation program should be sought rather than prison. Believing that many times is an escape hatch from reality and the institutional protective life style it provides, accentuating the problem rather than solving it.

Part IX: Times of My Life and Civil Disobedience

The thinking that goes on in my mind is one of giving more intensity to interest in people. Events, thinking, family and living is to get more done in a shorter period of time, to do it with gusto and meaning, giving credence to priorities—being God, family, life, friend and business.

To do in six weeks that which normally takes six months, by separating the wheat from the chaff. In the confines of prison there is a diverse cross section of mentalities and personalities. They range from the very embittered people, fired with hostility and aggressiveness, to the humble, passive and almost meek. As in a college fraternity, the mind, the personality, of one person would fit well into the syndrome of a certain kind of behavior, a higher affinity of certain kinds of unallowable behavior and activity in society. In my own case with an almost insatiable thirst of drive, a more than normal courting of disaster, taking chances that not even the best of odds makers would give.

The reason for this flamboyant behavior is founded in a need for activity with too much of a socialistic, hedonistic attitude engulfing one's life.

Today, March 8, is the eve of the most important phase of these last 90 days, sentencing. There were four fellow inmates in my cell who wanted to say a prayer for me before my day in court the following morning. The young black fellow, who is about 30, is the one who offered the prayers while I lay back on my bunk. The other three fellows kneeled by my bed. The prayer of "Please Lord look after Mr. Foster and let him be released tomorrow to go back to his family. I don't really know him but I feel he is a good man. Please let the judge show him mercy—You know what is going to happen. Please Dear Lord, let him go home. He has been like a father to me and helped me in many ways. I feel God sent him here to be with us."

Personalities knit in the confined block which is a hallway 30 feet long, a 9 x 9 dormitory cell with toilet, sink and shower end of hallway with a dayroom 20 x 15 feet large, with two metal tables and two metal chairs and a TV set. The cellmates range in age from 25 to 45, the average being about 30. Half are white and half are black, most of them are second and third time offenders for crimes like murder, rape, robbery, and breaking and entering. As always, my ability to adapt to various situations has been an asset. Due to the maximum security to which everyone is exposed, cooperation and amenable ways make things seem smoother than trying to rebel against the system.

Having been given the name "Fred", from the Flintstones, due to my short haircut as of this past week, projected my boyish look. My stickman is called "Barney". The days, weeks and months are orderly, sameness in a mechanical like fashion in dispensed orders, food; sleep (punishment hangs over your head always).

March 9, 1982—a date not to be forgotten. I was sentenced to two years in the state penitentiary for being a habitual offender (driving a car). The prosecutor asked for five years. The judge looked upon my driving record with disfavor although the two years' sentence was decided prior to my entering the courtroom. Letters and testimony were given on my behalf, as was my own apology for any indiscretion to the Commonwealth. The judge considered the past 90 days of incarceration as well as my being held without bond having devastating financial consequences.

Thinking that one was considered innocent until proven guilty, however, I was wrong. Being intrigued with how the system sometimes works improperly, as do the people who appear before it. The words "probable cause" cover the gamut of exercise of power and authority in sometimes not equitable judicial procedures. You will get process and if you are lucky you may get justice.

As the eleventh hour approaches, it is difficult to believe the reality of it all. You are faced in a cold and powerful way with a sentence from one to five years in the penitentiary that seems more stringent than two years in jail.

The thoughts coming thru my mind give new insights and prepare new complexities to the human thought process—such as what it takes to murder, to rape, to commit armed robbery is as frightening an act of crime for me as it would be for other inmates to drive a car on a revoked license.

It is noticed that the vegetation process seems to be a dominating event here: Dependency, lethargy and apathy take over from time to time. It is a challenge to keep the mind alert, fresh, and welcome clear thoughts. The mental and physical dominion of March 9th again ran the gamut of feelings. Apprehensive of the outcome was mild—the related mood was frightening in retrospect. I got caught up in the belly of the beast due to my taking unreasonable risks. While in here there are no restaurant bills, gasoline or alcohol expenses, wear and tear on shoes and clothing and external stresses are eliminated. Writing these thoughts, reflecting how one person who writes his letters in blood from his arm and spreads it on paper with a worn out pen, mailing it in his generic envelope and stamp provided by the jail. The human need to communicate is a thirsty one.

We are a product of our associations and genes. None of us is an island unto himself. Environment and experience is learned from bad and good judgment. The breath of fresh air, looking out the window is appreciated. Hoping, waiting for positive signs of release are important to maintaining evenness of mind.

The mind wanders back to years past and objectively evaluates relationships with the people who crossed your path. The effect of what that relationship was. How you thought of them and how they thought of you and what effect it had.

The poor judgment of driving into the lion's den daily became an ingrained habit as natural as drinking a glass of water. Being over anxious in my efforts to get bail after being put under arrest, my appearance in court coerced me not to give proper thought into establishing an adequate defense. The permissiveness of my lifestyle caused complications ranging from financial to personal. Everything we do is a chance. However, they must be weighed to possible consequences. Winston Churchill said, "we either learn from history or we are destined to repeat it."

The songs "*Gambler*", "*Nobody does it Better*" were so fitting to my lifestyle in the last few years. Today we live, for tomorrow we might die. I was inebriated with gusto and hedonism and the bon vivant, always reaching.

Experiences of a few months ago seem like a few years ago. The feeling you have thinking of those people close to you, your beloved wife, mother and children. To see their faces and hear their voice is longed for like a breath of fresh air into your very being.

The marking of time goes on as days turn into nights and back into days again. The outside seems so close yet so far removed. Inside these walls is a workhouse of bodies that have been slowed down physically, mentally and productively to a small percentage of what they were. However, the appreciation of one's freedom and the use of one's self discipline for his betterment of self, forever becomes the quest.

The floors, the rooms, the inmates are kept in the epitome of cleanliness. Shave and shower daily, three meals a day, library, once a week, recreation, twice a week, church on weekend, television all day long. Canteen twice a week, telephone once a week and visitors on 20-minute weekend visits, laundry twice a week and haircuts on request. The guards are your servants and butlers. Life is pre-planned and you are waited on hand and foot. No worries, full health treatment, no money has to be spent and there are no responsibilities. The homeless commit petty crimes to get into this robotic existence—the advantage of a warm bed, plenty of heat in your living area. There is a bright light for reading and cushions on the chair you sit on. Each dining table has its own clique for meals: the rapists, the faggots, the drug dealers, and the weirdoes.

Every day is marking a day, a nick in Father Time. The undisciplined, permissive, impersonal are the ones who created a pattern of petty thieving. The adroit 25–30 year old who developed a lifestyle of crime. The transition from one phase to the next is as easy as sunset following sunrise. Then there is the cold, impersonal and boldness of the individual who courts more serious offences such as murder and rape.

The feelings that are present within the confines of the building in Virginia Beach, is just a building that represents to many a psychological, as well as a physical hold—to another world. The kaleidoscopic feelings range in unison of relaxation escape from reality to a remorse, and a quest for what is right and good.

The revelation of the inner self is revealed by being cleansed in the months or years of confinement that have been meted out by a judge. Doing penance and having a contrite heart for one's misdeeds has a refreshing feeling in the balance of living. Often the person is sentenced for something other than a crime for which he is actually guilty. Ironically it sometimes produces a feeling of relief. A child who has disobeyed his parent is punished. To some it seems predestined.

Freak events may occur with the person found guilty and sentenced, but not guilty of said act. Then there is the 21-day rule, under which sentence is implemented and no further evidence can be introduced—how shameful! It is easier to accept and make the most of the situation than to have bitterness, rebellion and frustration as this will devour and strip you mentally and physically as piranha fish do their prey.

I perceived myself as a manipulative, permissive individual who had let improper behavior jeopardize my work, my living patterns that impacted adversely on family and personal fulfillment creating an entanglement of confusion.

It is interesting to note, however, that within the confines of the block honesty prevails—not going into another's room, leaving personal items about, borrowing and returning. "Never needed drugs to get high, did you?" "Always been on a high, moving like you have" was said to me by one of my fellow inmates. "Had I had been sent to the Eastern Shore of Virginia for eight months to be alone, it could have been disastrous" someone said to my wife.

It is a mere fact that if you walk in it long enough you are bound to get some of it on the soles of your shoes. I had been flirting with disaster for a long time, however, feeding off people made incarceration easy, like a game. Innocence or guilt often has little to do with the system. It is whether the prosecutor can outwit the defense or vice versa.

Medicine practices its games on the patient. The businessman has the general citizenry to promote his wares and the game of scams and promotion permeate the playground of life. Understand the lie is paramount in the business, political, legal and medical arena. The use of the lie should be our biggest concern for the 21st century.

June 1, 1982, transferred to Deep Meadows Correctional Center in handcuffs and leg irons. Out all day in sun, basketball on asphalt and tennis court—canteen purchase of almost anything daily. Bunks are laid-out in 12s in a trailer marked six on a side. Inmates have access to liquor and almost any kind of drug through accommodating guards.

Clothes like dungarees are cut with razor blade for shorts. Head count every day at 4:00 PM where you stand by your bed to be counted, lights out at 11:30 PM., must be outside every morning from 8:30–10:30 AM. Almost anything can be obtained within the population work camp.

Today, Wednesday, June 2, 1982 much like Tuesday. Everything here seems to be very loose with intimidation: Threat of penalty write-up is always permeating the climate of the place, which can consist of everything from loss of good time to isolation to add time.

The organized disorganization is an interesting paradox. There is an underlying sense of pride for many of personal neatness and cleanliness. Due to the physical layout of the sleeping quarters, shower and toilet facilities, one wonders about the sanitation of it all. The meager existence and the lack of good thinking, feeling and the demeaning surroundings even though the most aggressive people are thorzaned or pacified into a state of passivity due to the demoralizing conditions that prevail.

Thursday, June 3 thru June 7, Sunday—the feeling of drabness almost deliberate sullen look on faces and morose outlooks, attitudes that are pure survival blank. Days and nights move with unyielding motion. Friday and Saturday are almost identical to Thursday. Sunday separated by the most welcome visit of wife and son—an important and welcomed interlude in the dispassionate days that precede and follow, relieved by the physical outlet of exercise, by way of basketball, for an hour or so a day.

The abundance of freedom of motion, in contrast to limited personal activity is interesting. Once you can have almost full access to the outside it is taken too much for granted.

The lethargy, apathy, nothingness existence, blurred feelings of taste, smell and sound and for preservation are indeed great.

It seems the dictates of the parole officer carry unreasonable discretion and weight in dealing with parolees—what would be a violation by one parole officer would not be by another.

The desire for intelligent, stimulating conversation just as food for the body is needed so very much to steer away from lethargy, apathy and robot-like existence.

Humor, smiling and pieces of joy are so remote due to the darkness of the surroundings. I found my thinking likened to a scanner—experiencing everything from test pattern of not feeling to feelings of absurdity and ridiculousness of being caught up in nothingness. The waste, the overriding intimidation is beyond belief.

The makeshift living and existing in a suspended state of blah—all decisions of when to eat, sleep, where you go—are programmed for you.

Today is Saturday, June 12, 1982, 7:00 AM. My awakening daily between 6 and 6:30 AM for the last six months and going to bed between 10:00 and 11:15 PM is diametrically opposite to my life prior to these six months. Hopefully, this interlude in my life will soon be in the past—never to be repeated, but always to be remembered with tongue in cheek. There is much humor in the most tragic of events.

The shaving and use of hot water is coordinated with the shower, precipitated by hollering out, "hot water." Even the evangelist, under the guise of religion, manipulates the hearts and minds of men with his promises, draining the emotion of man to enrich his coffers consistently while feeding off his weak and susceptible prey.

My disregard for traffic laws in the state of Virginia was dealt with harshly and the phases that led to my incarceration were gauche but humorous. It was a penance for my permissive lifestyle of many years. This whole confinement was like a game of cops and robbers we played as children.

Today, a Tuesday morning: The thought of driving seems to be one easier solved in thought than in reality. Attempting to understand the feelings of my wife, Anne. What were they as we drove to New York, Richmond, Washington, and Charlottesville and throughout the Hampton Roads area? From October 2, 1980 to December 15, 1981, what were the feelings? Did I know or did she know the possible consequences of what could happen and did happen? It is hard to believe that "driving a car" could have such far-reaching ramifications.

Another routine day except for the unusual letter from my sister Pat who seems to have that touch of being so personal but also most impersonal at the same time—a trait that I myself feel guilty of. Feeling that if one could be emancipated 24 hours a week the impact of incarceration would be reduced a thousand fold. However, on the other side of the coin, 24 hours freedom after a few weeks would make incarceration psychologically ten times more difficult—an interesting paradox. It is a learning experience to feel and see your reaction to your incarceration for the first time in your life.

It is frightening to feel one's life is under the control of someone else's jurisdiction and the dichotomies of the law that you are a pawn. You want to maintain your respect for justice and right for your own inner peace and feelings that things are right and in order.

The judge, the courts have a true problem in dealing objectively to the law under this driving—traffic offense. Alcohol oriented, they too often have been guilty of driving under the influence whereas other felonies of robbery, forgery, embezzlement, murder, they can stand back and look at objectively.

The permanent feeling that is in my conscious self is the feeling of the increase of awareness of the outside world from flowers; air, trees, rain, sun and people increases a thousand fold. Here we are 135 days later—four bond hearings, one trial, one sentencing—no bond: three lawyers and another step in the twilight zone.

It is Saturday afternoon. The cell is like the hotel block at Virginia Beach except there is a window with no bars and a screen. Fresh air and sunlight come through. Having been here two days now, the place is laid out like the Monticello Arcade with three tiers. It is a processing reception center run mechanically and efficiently, anticipating release within a fortnight.

Being honest with myself—I feel badly about the blatant bad judgment of driving and taking extremely high odds on my driving and being arrested. This unfortunate event was inevitable. This caution was put to the winds.

Life in prison is a naked unyielding force, unrelenting where equality though is probably more fair than any society or civilization on earth. It is disciplined and a boldness of truth is staggering yet the system of punishment is many ways archaic, but the best we have found in the last 1,000 years. It probably is this fundamental stark truth that has in its favor a dispassionate truth of dealing with the problem of society that has been one of the least yet most tampered gifts of justice and retribution that have passed down by our forefathers.

To get in a matter of speaking, into your inner self is important. There is an underlying humor of driving a car—not driving a car. Saying to the honorable judge of the circuit court today, "I was late due to the fact I had trouble starting my car"—pun. He finally smiled and said, "That went over my head."

I was asked today how it felt to be eating with a murderer, a robber and a common thief. Eating at the "college table," one fellow graduated from Temple, another from University of Florida and the other from Old Dominion University. Dreaming last evening that I was sentenced to life and 83 years for kidnapping all the judges in my van and driving them all over hell and back, getting them totally inebriated whereby only one judge survived saying repeatedly, "life and 83 years for you Big Guy."

The fun times of trying to get the policeman who stopped me to give up his car and drink with me was interesting. Surprised that he did not give me a ticket for driving under the influence or assaulting him as I amicably put my arms around his neck to give him a hug. Remembering the judge who found me innocent was an old William and Mary ball boy and creator of the Alcohol Safety Action Program in Tidewater, Virginia, the judge had asked, "Did we win?" He gave me the benefit of the doubt on my .10 blood alcohol reading. The attorney previously retained, I discharged due to his improper grammar while instructing me in a circuitous route to his office. He later became the Commonwealth's attorney and was sentenced to jail for his repeated DUI offences.

Comment this evening was how long had I been married: 24 years, have three children in college. Another said, "You had better slow down."

The ominous feeling of living where I do, which came about over 12 years ago, in the southernmost point of Virginia Beach, was more of luck, timing and Irish stroke. My ultimate in good judgment was meeting my wife, Anne.

My fascination with the inner workings of the mind tells me that travels through life are an exciting odyssey. Remember the scarecrow in the Wizard of Oz when asked, "how do I get there" replied, "this way" pointing in all directions is analogous to our everyday living. Whatever route we probably "will get there," taking the most enjoyable and interesting route possible. Feeling this was a pre-destined move, as we are is the sum product of our associations, environment and genes. There is uniqueness in every person and event. What is done today can have impact on one month, one year from now. The saying, *when we are green we grow, but when we think we are ripe we begin to get rotten*, is reflected in business, love, working and learning experiences—there is no standing still—either you are moving forward or backward.

Destinies of lives and of nations have been shaped by what is thought. Aristotle's *Rhetoric* teaches this in Ethos—Pathos—Logos. To walk in another's shoes—to deal emotionally, but always logically with what happens.

It is an obligation to understand this responsibility to ourselves and to know ourselves through this we have more appreciation, which helps us to understand the masters in art, literature, and music. To know a Michelangelo existed, a Galileo, an Einstein—find what most influenced their lives. Example is the most powerful thing on earth. There is a statement I will always remember: "Watch how you live for you may be the only Bible some people will ever read."

There is a saying that applies to many aspects of our life and how we live it. *When that One Great Scorer comes to call upon your name, it is not that you won or lost it is how you played the game*—Grantland Rice. It is not always winning it is in losing it teaches us how to overcome handicaps. For this overshadows the best of wins because the lesson is better taught. Discovering this through my incarceration was in some ways a blessing in disguise, making me appreciate life and living more in the increased awareness of maximizing my talent, my thinking and my time.

Driving for forty years had been my security blanket psychologically as the habits developed have been part of my being—my psyche—so interwoven into my lifestyle and thinking. It was hard to separate myself from it. It was a catalyst to other aspects of my living such as thinking, playing, eating, sleeping and being in the loop.

Part X:
Deep, Deep Reflections

There is a thought that expresses feeling and insight into genetic strains and it goes as follows:

The Americans are proud of what they can accomplish—not what they can learn. The Swiss are proud of what they can learn—not what they can accomplish. The Greeks are proud to be a man. The French are proud to be. The English get caught up in their bloodline. The Italians are full of emotion, making their sculptures of gods look like men—the Greeks make their sculptures of men look like gods. The Irish are the smartest, the most charming and the best looking. It is said that if it were not for whiskey they would own the world.

Assets are born out of liabilities. Fortunately, every man, consciously or not, brings something different to the table due to his uniqueness as a human being because of this great quality thinkers, poets, philosophers; musicians, scientists and artists are made. Their own passion and the influence of men who have come before them have made them a captain of their own fate. As Shakespeare said, "The fault, dear Brutus is not in the stars, but in ourselves that we are underlings"—Julius Caesar.

Nexus, meaning connection, everything has two sides as well as a third side as in a coin we don't see, however it has a deeper meaning. Let us go back to when we were children when we wanted to do something and our parents would not give in to our desires. It seemed that the more we screamed the more adamant our parents were. Now if we would back off and show not such an intense demand our parents would have been able to assess the situation and logically concede to our wishes if it was in our best interest. On the other side if we deceptively hide our emotions and pretend it is not important that our demands be fulfilled, we are using another dimension that on the surface seems quite smart, however it has the potential to do harm in other areas in negotiating our life quest ironically this is intellectual dishonesty.

Life presents many interesting thoughts, feelings and actions taken. My beginning relationship with the mother of my four children born outside of my marriage was borne out of curiosity and fascination which ironically are the factors which brought me into the life insurance business in June 1956 for a successful business life for over 40 years.

The living on the edge syndrome that seems to come forth—pushing the envelope—was created in November 1958 on my meeting a young, sweet, innocent Navy nurse who was to become, fortunately or unfortunately, a big part of my life for the next 20 years.

The emotions ran the gamut of feelings and affected many lives, in many ways will forever take paths our lives took that were altered for evermore. I honestly regret the grief and sadness I brought to so many lives and the lack of the fulfillment of my nurse friend to be all she could be saddens me.

John Steinbeck wrote, "There is a room of experience we cannot and most will not ever enter." The dynamics of the three adult principals were so synchronized to make us enter this room of experience. If any one of us were changed by the slightest neuron this experience would never have been and endured for so long. The relationship with my loving wife, Anne, and myself has been made stronger, healthier and happier because of this room of experience that was entered and survived. Had this experience occurred twenty years later, vengeance and cynicism could replace innocence.

My mind has always been in the curious and fascinating realm. Initially in my 20s on entering the life insurance business, I saw a business that enabled me to do business with whom I wanted, when I wanted and how I wanted while meeting an array of people in different walks of life with different backgrounds. How I used my time and imagination was up to me. Imagination, however, has its own nemesis. My virgin ways until I married ironically in some ways had a positive impact on my life.

Part XI:
Karma of People and Thinking

Have you ever noticed that certain kinds of people work in certain jobs and are a mirror of their jobs or careers? It has been my feeling that aggressive people are fitted by temperament to do better in such positions as doctor/surgeon, lawyers/criminal, salesman/minister. Shakespeare said, "All the world is a stage and the men and women in it are merely players"—As You Like It. Analytical people seem to mirror jobs such as internists, scientists, and accountants. They usually are articulate and painstaking in their thinking. Conversely, the amicable are politicians, librarians, waiters and clowns. The librarians are most genuine, the politicians and waiters are driven often by pseudo friendliness due to their vested interest. Clowns and politicians seem analogous, however the clown is there genuinely to amuse—not to conspire and to be self-serving and gain favor by dubious means. Going on to the expressive we find artists, actors, poets and writers. We are most consistent with our personalities and are uncomfortable out of our designated zones.

Connecting with reality for many people is a hard thing to do. Recently saw a movie depicting a little town where everything is pleasant but is out of touch with where the world is, it was a Shangri-La with no such thing as pain, rain or flowers and all is black and white. Emotions did not exist and all is good and all is constant. Weather, thinking, work and all life is structured. As a young person I witnessed some of this with people close to me. All was good, pleasant and patronization was at a feverish pitch.

Having a sense of belonging and having a routine is important, however when it becomes an end all it will consume you and you won't know it is happening to you. Striving for psychic income is doing what makes you happy, however in my case it has to be constructive, enjoyable and interesting.

There must be a mutual trust; if it falters it has to be resuscitated in order to make for a happy outcome, if not, it wilts like a flower on a bush that does not get enough sunshine or rain. Thinking back on my own life with my beloved wife—it is the depth of connection, experiences and feeling that have helped mold a certain beauty that could not be achieved separately—it is both of us seeing beyond to the mutual fulfillment of each other—our destiny for now and the years to live ahead. I honestly believe that the best is yet to come. The mentality of two is there and the wisdom and the passion for life are overwhelming.

Influences and genetic strains are why we like hunting, fishing or why we are indifferent to it. Likes and dislikes are created. Feeling before we are born our mother/father's disease and health are a part of us.

Interesting that my mind works like the gears in a car: When in neutral I am on hold, in first gear revving-up, second gear the motor is getting stronger, third gear I am moving out with lots of thoughts and feelings honing in. Fourth gear is the ultimate gear and fifth gear is out-of-control, as the mind cannot keep up with the plethora of excited senses. Alcohol can be a catalyst to good thinking, good music and good smells and breathtaking views.

The Irish disease can be a blessing or a curse. Drinking can be an asset or a problem. It is all in our attitude and our genes. We are a compilation of neurons; our own wellbeing is essentially being true to our feelings and ourselves.

People like to say, "Yes" rather than "No", as no has a negative affect on them. Saying yes makes one feel better. Conversely, not showing up, being late becomes a habit that reflects into how we conduct our daily lives. One's dialogue and reaction can be trickled down to these habits. The ways we act in one area of our life is how we respond in other areas.

If we were all alike it would be a boring world, yet one with chaos and conflict. However, we are unique and this paradox still exists. Why? The slight difference in every organism interacting with another brings to this earth a fascinating odyssey in what happens every second that we are alive. The peoples of the world are ingrained with their sense of tradition, their likes and dislikes, which are influenced by their environment, their genes. Why would God create some of his creatures with innate evil, others with innate goodness? Is it because He wants to keep a certain balance in His creation? Or can the bad learn from the good to lead more fulfilling lives. Why? The scholars and scientists have pontificated this matter for eons of time. Why do some of us feel better when we do for others? The reason is that it makes us feel better by dividing ourselves thereby multiplying ourselves. Why is it others feel servitude and less when they do for others? It is because of lack of self, their own self-worth. It is vital to feel like somebody—not to be somebody, to feel worthy. There is a thin line between free will and predestination. It is often an excuse for our actions by using this Presbyterian theory. Watch out for self-fulfilling prophecies that can fit into our ultimate ends. Why do some of us lead a charmed life and others are strewn with frustration, disease? Life is a perpetual quest. Is it genes or are we a mirror of our thoughts and actions? Medical studies reflect this thinking. It is our environment, the books we read and our associations.

I thought as a small child that "curiosity and fascination" have been my driving force in living and asking "why." Why would I let my raging hormones put myself and others in a situation that was so compelling, self-hypnotizing and only death would have stopped me from pursuing my quarry—why? Through use of my wits, my inimitable gall seemed to transcend into my business life. My gargantuan appetite in some ways was consuming me, however it was keeping me alive and razor sharp. There is a tapestry of living: my mother was one of nine children, two died, one as a baby the other as an adult. I had nine children, one dying as a baby and the other as an adult. Is this happening out of design or is this a power that is hidden and unbeknownst to us? I look to myself and ask why? Why would I pursue, with such unrelenting force, where did this come from? Generations before me perhaps!

I ask why do most human beings enjoy, whether it is in the realm of medicine, religion, business, being lied to? Hearing the truth seems so impersonal, cold and not as exciting as the lie. Is it because as children they liked the fantasy world they were imbued with that gives them a pseudo security blanket, like in the cartoon "Peanuts" by Charles Schulz or in the nursery rhymes they heard when they were very young.

Part XII:
Looking Back Again

Relating back many yesterdays when a close friend John died: Remembering his smile and his sense of humor, evoking a certain sense of humor in me that nobody before or since has done. Oh what a good feeling! His comments, such as "we should start a club and name it Last Man Standing"—to qualify you have to consume a fifth of whiskey every other day, eat at least two full lobster dinners each week and take two two-week vacations a year to some far off isle and report back to other club members quarterly your stories and times. Couple this with good music, good sights, good thinking and good actions that others can learn and gain by. You are now in touch with the magic buttons of living.

For now I know that for $1,000,000 or $10,000,000 a year I would not work at a job eight to ten hours a day because I would be unable to do and see the things for which I have passion. Fully aware twelve years into the future is just a few minutes of time—oh precious time. Life is so beautiful, and can be so rewarding. There is much that we can do for others and self that is mind expanding. Reflecting back 40 years and beyond, remembering my key to the Playboy Club and my new Jaguar as the only assets I had, except for my mind, my wife, my Irish luck, my unbelievable imagination and energy. Of course these were mighty big assets to carry forth. Looking back on some of my life's saga here goes. Remembering September 1977 in Chicago when I met an older gentleman whom I had heard about for many years—a leading insurance guru in the United States. After much waiting I seized the opportunity to speak with him when he was alone. Hearing about him since my first entering the insurance business I proceeded to engage him in conversation for the next three and a half hours into the wee hours of the morning. Never has so much good thinking come my way, particularly in the ratio of time spent. On returning home I sent a note telling how much I had enjoyed meeting and being with him. He promptly sent me a posty note on my letter, which I still have. His note said, "I have never met anybody who meets people quicker and easier than you. Thank you for your letter."

Reflecting on the strange ironies of life once at the local Holiday Inn I was scheduled to meet a physician client who did not show up. I sat at the bar for the next six hours drinking rum and Cokes, 20 of them. At the end of the evening asking soberly the bartender what I owed, he replied, "you do not owe me anything, I feel that I owe you—now I have seen it all." Remembering another time with my more than one encounter with the police and the courts for being a concrete cowboy. It was late one evening a policeman stopped me for going too slow. I went to his patrol car to open the door to get him out. He asked if I had been drinking. I replied, "of course I have" as he approached my vehicle. I said "See the half gallon of whiskey on the back seat." Then putting my arms around his neck in an amicable way I asked him to park his car across the street at the gas station and come with me. Smiling humorously he turned around to get back in his patrol car without ever giving me a summons and said, "Try to be careful." Another time, while being in court in a neighboring city, for a DUI offense, I caught the presiding judge's eye as I entered the courtroom that I hadn't seen in almost 30 years. On approaching the bench he asked the policeman if I cooperated with license, etc. The officer said, "Yes, but his breath reading was over the limit." The judge asked me where had I been and I said that I was coming home from a William and Mary football game. He asked, "Did we win?" I responded, "Yes." He then said, "I am going to give you the benefit of the doubt—case dismissed." Ironically the attorney, who was going to represent me, I had discharged because of his misspelled words and improper grammar in a letter he

Part XII: Looking Back Again

had sent. The judge, strangely enough, had been the ball boy for the William and Mary basketball team and remembered me, it was that look in his eye. This same judge was the initiator of the Alcohol Safety Action Program in the Hampton Roads area. I later learned that the attorney was cited with DUI (driving under the influence of alcohol).

There was another time in this same era when my driver's license was revoked and I was stopped for driving and appeared before the judge with another person's driver's license, unbeknownst to the court. The judge informed me that another Conn, the name on the license that I was using, had been in court for a DUI charge the week before. After the day's court session ended, he asked me to come to his chambers behind the court room and he said to me "since we are no longer in court who are you really?" I told him who I was. We chatted and laughed and shortly thereafter left the building together. My car was parked next to his, which was assigned to another judge. As I followed him out of the parking area, with no license in my name we accidentally ended up at the same drug store a few miles away at which I purchased a best seller paperback book entitled "Looking Out After #1," which I shared with my friend the judge.

All of these are strange anomalies that I have been able to observe and have been part of from my business life to my living in general.

Remembering times when Sheldon Kelly, the writer assigned by Warner Brothers, came by my home and was introduced to Anne, my wife, saying that Warner Brothers wanted to do a movie on my life. Her comment, "Certainly." At that same time, as if orchestrated, the home phone rang in the room where we were standing and the caller said, "May I speak to Donald Foster—this is Warner Brothers calling". She handed the phone to me and within minutes the business line rang which she answered to hear, "This is Theron Raines, Donald Foster's agent." When we later met Theron Raines we learned that he also was the agent for Sophia Loren as well as James Dickey, author of Deliverance, a film starring Bert Reynolds and Jon Voight. For the next six months the writer, Sheldon Kelly, was with me until I was incarcerated, taping conversations with friends, business associates and members of my family on the saga of my life.

These most interesting experiences were in the early 80s. It brought forth feelings of anger, humor, accented by love, and dedication. Adventures had more of a bonding feeling that we had survived. Never to be forgotten are the bonding experiences of friends and just-mets. Remembering my friend, Otis Sistrunk, the all pro football player from the 70s who I met at the Norfolk YMCA,—when I asked Otis to come with me in my car after a workout at the Y, his comment was, "I would be afraid to get in a car with you and ride to the end of the block." I said, "Look at you, 320 pounds, bald, black head!" He replied, "You know Don you have a way of mesmerizing people." Then he said, "What time do we leave?"

Learning and thinking are food for the brain as meat and potatoes are food for the body. This gives pleasure in living and enlarges the circle of life, increasing the appetite for living and its wonderful adventures and challenges.

Looking back into the 50's and 60's, a millionaire was not commonplace. Ironically there are more people today who have large incomes in ratio to a generation ago, however they have incurred large debts and a morass of entanglements. The possibility of spiraling out of control is due to their not understanding values. This is a style that transcends into many areas of life, from medicine, law, to politics, to religion that has superceded substance in our daily lives. When foundations crumble society crumbles.

Looking back on this day, March 15, 1979, it seems only a few months ago—not 23 years. This is the day Patrick O'Sullivan Foster, my father, died. Looking at the years to come, twenty years hence, it is exciting, however frightening—I will be 90—my wife 86. If I could ask for one thing it would be the power to help and heal others spiritually, mentally and physically.

A good friend, Buck Cowling, gave the following passage to me several months before he died at age 81. He said that he had written it as a high school student.

Life is like a flickering candle flame—when each and every organism is called forth upon the stage to play out the role of its given name. But like the flame that shall flicker and die and cease to exist within the human eye. Man is but a molecular structure occupying space—electric circuit operating on a 20 to 2000 micro-volt emotional circuit according to the emotional level of the organism. Constructed as a whole by the symbolic logic that has been programmed in him from birth until time we put forth a question to Him. I shall be forever in the minds of those I have known. Man is in a constant change. The only absolute is change. Pass it on!

Part XIII:
Reflections

Looking back over my life after leaving high school, never again to play football, baseball or poker. I am thankful that my interest in playing basketball accelerated thru college to even until a few years ago when, due to an arthritic hip, came to a halt. Tennis, which I played as a teenager, still remains on a limited basis, however I never had that competitive spirit with it. Coming to realize as I approach my 68th year, the things I do today will most likely disappear from my life in the next decade and half, like tennis, drinking with my buddies, traveling long distances and the simple art of driving a car out of the local area.

Must ask myself at the end of day, "Am I satisfied with how I traded my time today?" Tomorrow brings interesting thoughts to mind and today becomes tomorrow by how you live. Yesterday is our teacher as well as our memory. Emotions often lead us to places our minds wouldn't ever go. Knowing my connection with the mother of four of my children for over 20 years was born out of memories and symbols. The memory was my childhood experiences of uncle's two nurse friends and even as a teenager my affinity for nurses, with their blue capes and uniforms, "the all-American look" became an obsession. Wondering now and then, connections made as a child, a student, and many as an adult are temporary. Liking and not seeing again, friends of 40 or 50 years ago, even if they live in the same area, why? Symbols of common interests and associations make lasting impressions on your mind as in the "nurse syndrome" mentioned earlier. For example with childhood associations we are reticent to recreate feelings of long ago because there is no longer common bonding. We are secure most often where we are and don't want to resurrect old memories even if they were good at the time. Thinking strong linkage is not there, fading in desire to maintain the connection. It is not knowledge, but affairs of the heart that cause disruption. Reckless abandon can be found in love as in war where judgment has gone awry. Gut feelings should be our guide.

The hawk, I feel, is similar in some ways to myself as it and I get focused and intense on what I am doing, never looking back to protecting my back. Knowing I would not go bankrupt, divorce or even change careers, understanding this now affectively because of my own self worth. Many times we live in a fantasy world trying to escape reality; however if you know your heart you know what is going to happen most times. This is not a psychic ability; it is more knowing what we are made of.

When my mind is set on doing something, it is so intent that judgment does not prevail regardless of the risk. Becoming so focused on accomplishing the task at hand, like the hawk zeroing in on it's prey. There are advantages and disadvantages to this mindset. It has been my experience with the things and people we dislike that we are merely seeing ourselves. The chief aspect of my triangular moves in life on reflecting could have changed the outcome of many people's lives. Had my wife or my friend engaged in an affair, knowing not whether I would have been able to cope? Fortunately, this did not happen. My boring into people and situations has been a two-edged sword. It served me well in my business as I maximized personal relationships and intellectual interactions. Zeroing in on thoughts, things, places and people, I was relentless in my pursuit. Conversely, the downside of this, intimidates, frightens, often counterproductive, leaving the prey in flight. I have had a pied piper syndrome and a Peter Pan approach to living, seeing it as an adventure.

This past week on leaving a music program at a private school, I happened to look behind me. Seeing a white-haired woman, I first did not recognize; she smiled and said, "Quite a surprise seeing you here.

How is your leg?" I replied, "Much better thank you." Later realizing that I had spent many moments with this woman and she had given birth to four of my children. Her look seemed to say, "Don, you are a big lovable bear"—we all know that. My relationship with her reminded me of the line, "These are the times that try men's souls."

Will Rogers often said, "I never met a man I didn't like—if not I must get to know him better." There is bad in the best of us and good in the worst of us. The problem is that we quickly judge and it is hard to change. Personally it has been annoying, but curious, that people say that they will be someplace or will do this or that and often they have no intention of following through. Cancellations, changes, not keeping one's word have made me realize the time that I have here on earth is being sabotaged and I must avoid or bypass these situations—mentally and physically with humor. Thinking back to my college days in Williamsburg and days when I dated nurses who were in my hometown Portsmouth. In the beginning the nurse I pursued usually was not there because she had to work, forgot, or simply didn't show up. After a while I made dates with two or three nurses at approximately the same time. I would then go to my first choice, if not there the second, then the third. Usually being assured of one showing up, I would change the others. Never realizing that this was going to be presented to me in my life's work as well as social meetings where the person was either not there because they forgot or had to work, or chose not to show up. This exercise of appointment making amid changes and no-shows cost me untold hours of time that I need not have used in such pursuit. I honestly know that I could have done in 10 years what it took 40 years to accomplish in my business by applying the fundamental corrections that I did as a college student.

I feel most men don't think. Knowing that the opposite of courage is not cowardice but conformity. Keeping the mind focused on its wishes it would be impossible to fail at anything we attempt. We are what we think about all day long. This is why it is necessary to watch what we do, think; feel, say and with whom we associate because this is what we are becoming.

As I write these words I am feeling how short life is. I have felt this way for the last decade but now the feelings are clearer and stronger. There have been friends younger and older than myself who by sickness or accident have died. This in part is responsible for my thinking. I have watched friends who have lost much or their seeing and hearing and even their ability to walk—being wheelchair bound because of strokes or accidents. The upside of these observations and thinking has caused a sudden outburst of feeling of becoming a voracious reader, increasing my intensity, my awareness and sensitivity to nature, thoughts and people. This has deepened far greater than I could have imagined. Recently I came across the words "ethical will" and realized that much of the thinking in this book is this. An ethical will goes back to Jacob 3,000 years ago as his children gathered around his death bed and he shared his thinking and ideas of living as to enable them to live more rewarding and fulfilled lives. I am acutely aware there are things that I did and some things I should not have, however the learning experiences have been actual assets and they have strengthened my resolve. My pursuit of what is important to myself and my children and grandchildren is a worthy mission.

Part XIV:
Lifetime of Gleanings—Living on the Edge

A ship's bell was mounted firmly on a two-by-four pole in my family's backyard, which could be heard from four blocks away when I was beckoned for lunch, supper and for the late evening coming home from across the creek. The bell ringing was different for each occasion reminding me of Paul Revere's ride announcing the British are coming, one by land two by sea.

Bells, it seems, have been ringing ever since. Life has been an adventure and constantly on my mind is the childhood riddle, "Row, row, row your boat gently down the stream. Merrily, Merrily, merrily, life is but a dream." Curiosity and fascination is with me now more than ever. During the generation of the 40s through the 50s, children were given nicknames by their peers that were intriguing and appropriate, who were unique in themselves without these unusual monikers: Squirrel, Duck, Pole Cat, Mush Mouth, Slut King, and Poochie Dog, hearing today like 50 years ago, my friend the Slut King being asked, "King, who are you dating?" His reply then, as well as now, "anybody who will date me," being married six times, sometimes dressing as a male, sometimes as a female at the wedding altar. For example, Squirrel resembled a real squirrel and Poochie Dog looked like a real dog, their mannerisms and habits of eating and thinking were like the animals they represented. The Duck, for example, (which was me) didn't look like a duck, didn't walk like a duck and didn't talk like a duck, but you would find yourself trying to duck the duck because he was persistent in his ways, moving on his quarry relentlessly whether it be for business or just for fun. There was no such thing as his taking no for an answer. It seems childhood is a microcosm of our adult life. There was "Mush Mouth" who had probably the filthiest mouth of anyone I ever knew, slobbering four letter words constantly. At age 16 "Mush Mouth" said that he had to disassociate with us to become a minister—which he did—far left living seems often to be one of the keys to entering the ministry. However, after several marriages and divorces his stint with the ministry ended. It seems when we see one go so far to the left that he has to go right or end up dead, like intelligence—you can overload, your education begins to exceed your capabilities and you become something of an idiot.

There are certain instances we recall in our lives when we could have had our early demise and only circumstances saved us. A memorable situation occurred when some friends, who fought in the Korean war, asked me to stop by and have a beer one summer evening. After leaving my fiancée's home, because of the late hour I did not stop. The next morning their pictures were on the front page of the local newspaper for holding their parents hostage for sixteen hours with machine guns and other weapons. The National Guard had to come, roping off the neighborhood with no one entering or leaving until the brothers were disarmed. Ironically, the older brother majored in Greek mythology at the University of Virginia, which told me something about his psyche. The worst of these "on the edge" situations was a few years before when I was about 13 years of age, I played Russian roulette with a childhood friend with a pistol found in my father's garage—the last time I ever shot a pistol. The pistol misfired and I received the worst beating of my life with a leather belt from my father as he awoke me from a sound sleep. Speaking of "don't throw me into the briar patch" somehow these experiences of where I really wanted to be.

My experiences with unusual people and situations seem always to be there with me. The situation that frightened me the most happened when I was seventeen years old and a state highway employee because I was more aware of the danger, it was more frightening than my Russian roulette episode. A college friend of mine who was working with me at the time began harassing me with his sarcastic comments. There was a deep hole in the ground near where we were talking with 12 inch steel spikes pointing up. I came close to shoving him into this pit that the restraint hurt my right arm for the next day or so. Had I done this it would have impacted on my life for these past 50 years. After college a new life unfolded with analogous challenges and experiences.

The life insurance business and musings of the mind became my lifetime pursuit, a conduit for other life experiences. My education was my recreation, my play was my work, and my work was my play. Being the proud father of nine, I believe that sexual magnetism is a wonderful gift, but it cannot stand alone. Your thinking has to be below and above the belt if not you are in for much frustration, psychologically and financially. By choice or chance, I was able to overcome this adversity to self by attempting to have my cake and eat it too. Standing apart from my feelings and the situation—it is as if I were there but not there, living subjectively not objectively. I was a walking dichotomy mentally and morally. I could be more serious, yet more playful than anyone. Teaching others by being a good example I discovered incalculable psychic income and that made me become more of a person.

In relating to the smart, interesting people, the connecting line is a certain confidence and purpose of living life to the fullest. They are the people with the greatest imaginations and are the happiest people drawing big circles having interesting thoughts and are focused in what they want from being alive. My ten best friends are sincere, honest and can stand up and be counted. They are loyal, caring and it is fun to be in their company. Conversely, the biggest "assholes" I have ever encountered are entrenched either with the small man or Napoleonic syndrome, having one glaring characteristic: they are handicapped by a mass of insecurity and arrogance.

My final thought on a lifetime of gleaning and living on the edge is I remember clearly the conception of my oldest daughter and second oldest son—the kind of day, the mood experienced. Wondering if there is a link between how individuals in the act of love feel that has an impact on the organism that is conceived. Orgasm shapes organism. It is said the way we come into the world is, "Huh—huh" and the way we leave the world is, "Huh". I have discovered affectively now it is what happens in between that matters. Everything seems to be woven in a tapestry of thought.

Thinking of my life's choices during my mid-twenties and early thirties that resulted in nine children. My actions were overwhelmed by honest emotion and passion driven that knew no boundaries. All children are healthy, physically and mentally, except for two—one my daughter Suzanne who died at eleven days old and my son who died with a fatal asthmatic attack at age 27. It never crossed my mind to have any child aborted, in some strange way knowing that these children were supposed to be born.

People are the best highs possible, creating a feeling through the human exchange that can take your breath away, bringing out feelings in you that you did not know existed. Many of us have hang-ups that get in our way. It is most helpful to understand our passions. One, who unleashes his feelings and thinking, whether by music, art or simply living, is a most fortunate man.

There are some thoughts like people and ideas that have immeasurable value. Remembering my high school crush, I was so bashful I was unable to ask her for a date. Calling her on the telephone; I would hang up upon her answering. My basketball coach told me, "If you do not ask her to the junior-senior prom, I will ask her myself". He did and they went to the prom, because of this he lost his job. I still remember her address and telephone number and that was over fifty years ago. It is memories like this that seem so fresh. Many years ago a friend from out-of-town, spent a few days in my home. He went with me to the local YMCA. After our exercise regimen we went to lunch, joined by a fellow sports advocate who asked, "Why do you work with the doctors at the Naval Hospital and then play basketball with us?" My friend responded, "Don plays with the doctors and works with you". Memories themselves are so precious as time seems to race. The happenings of 10–20 years ago seem like the blink of an eye: my first date, my first movie. Those emotional feelings for the opposite sex are memories to be treasured. Things in my life like my first bike—I would not sell for any amount of money. The early memories of the Blue Ridge Mountains, Skyline Drive with my parents, the circuses, the local baseball games—they have a nostalgia that is irreplaceable. Sunshine on my face, playing baseball as a child, at the beach and the winds and rain on my face in a late spring shower are all what make up my psyche. Looking upon everything and everybody I have ever met as an investment—even if this investment goes sour, the experience itself enriches my being.

Looking back and meeting good people who have a comfortable fit with you is like a good book that you want to keep in your library and read over and over again. Opposites attract, because, ironically, it is the dissimilarities that make the similarities. We are a mass of contradictions; it is often the liabilities that are the assets. When liabilities don't convert to assets it is a defect of the genes, as in homosexuality to mental retardation. Observing most often that it is how you play games, tennis, golf, basketball; it is how you live your life—tentatively, defensively or aggressively. What you are thinking about and what you do you are again and again.

Concerned over our son's delayed development, the physician told my wife and me that our son had Hurler's disease and that he needed to go to Duke University Hospital in North Carolina for further studies. Responding that I would like to take him to the "pediatrician's pediatrician," his reply was "John is a good boy." Had I listened only to him my son probably would have died in childhood. He compensated for his special learning disabilities many ways by his unique outlook on life. Reminding me of the physician who told me that I had an asthmatic condition which could only be treated properly by going to the Duke Medical Center. However, I discovered that he was treating me with sulfur drugs and my medical entourage assured me that I had to break the attack of asthma with aminophilin and then treated with a ten-day antibiotic, which took care of the problem.

One of the unusual happenings with doctors in my life was a close friend with whom I weekly played tennis. After playing for several years and trading equal wins and losses, we decided to have a final match before his departure from the Navy. He had established a five-to-one advantage in the third set. Seeing the determined smug expression on his face, I mustered the adrenaline to bring the set to five-five. What proceeded was a sudden death playoff, a final game that enabled me to knock him down with my serve knocking the racquet out of his hand for a victory. That evening he had dinner at my home before leaving for Florida, that being the last time I ever saw him. He canceled $1,000,000 worth of life insurance due to our tennis experience.

Remembering three friends who committed suicide in the past dozen years; one was a high school friend, the other two insurance peers. In each case they seemed to show a happy face, however it was cloaked underneath in depression. It was difficult to know who they really were. They presented a friendly warm likeable manner, but deep down you knew that something was missing. These feelings carry over from your playing basketball to investing in the stock market. You image where you want to go and what is going to happen and more often than not it will be as you think and act. Somehow childhood experiences are mirrors of what is experienced years later. My organizing a baseball team at age 12 and being the captain, owner, pitcher/first baseman is probably not dissimilar 20 years later of creating my own financial consortium with a stockbroker, accountant and real estate broker affiliated where I was "chairman of the board." In both situations they were loosely made consortiums that assisted me in accomplishing my playful and business ends. My interest in people and the dynamics that make things happen in life and business has always been at the pinnacle of curiosity and fascination. This is what brought me into selling life insurance as an opportunity to meet people and be involved in situations on my terms. These experiences have helped me to understand and appreciate the beauty of life and its people. Knowing well that how I analyze my life helps me to understand the ups and downs better. The simple pluses are sometimes the minuses and the minuses are the pluses. It's like a fascination that I had for the life insurance business forty-seven years ago that kept it at that level of excitement until the last few years. Mirroring some times in my relationships with people—too persistent, overwhelming, however dogged determination has been relentless in accomplishing my objectives.

To My Children:

The text of this preachment is: Be at pains to see, hear or watch—and maybe buy—the best. That does not at all imply that one must be, or try to be a redwood tree, or a DaVinci. Therein lies frustration and maybe ulcers. But it does a buck good to see redwoods and it does me good to know a man like DaVinci existed.

Babson, the investment counselor, was often asked: "What is the best investment?" And he replied—"you". "And the next best?" "Your children." All of the great prophets have said the same; that is, the most important thing in the world is one's own development—the becoming more of a person. Of course, that is the theme of the great book, HUMAN DESTINY.

So—it is well that one sees, hears, watches and maybe owns what one can, of the best.

Unfortunately, one gets old before the lesson is learned, unless parents, spouses, teachers or friends lead toward it. For example, suppose I had not been led to see and hear Pavarotti or Sir Lawrence Olivier at his best, the best.

Or again, suppose I had not been encouraged to learn something of the beauty and craftsmanship of antique furniture. Consider the patience and preciseness with which the masters worked. Can I not use some of that?

Or again, suppose someone had not helped me to some appreciation of art. Would I have taken time from a busy convention to visit the National Galleries or the Smithsonian? And thereby have happy memories, be a bigger and better person.

Mother introduced me to good books. I have spent a lot of money and time on books since then. She also assured interest in good music. So what is a home without some good books and a piano?

Father exposed me to kindness and generosity. It took ten years after his death to appreciate the lesson. And the lesson becomes unlearned easily. Out of all lessons it has probably been the most useful and lovely, and age merely brings it into sharper perspective.

There are great plays and great books I have not read. You read them. There are great musicians and athletes I shall never see. You see them. There are great pictures I shall not see and most I could not appreciate—You see them and learn enough to appreciate them.

It has been said that the greatest single step in man's history was when he discovered right and wrong and that he had a choice. It may also be said that man takes a great step forward when he discovers mediocrity and greatness and that he has a choice as to what he will se and hear and maybe be.

You can see in any town or city or on farms tumbledown, unpainted houses with littered yards and sagging fences. All is ugly. There is no beauty. What is this? Is it that the occupants have not been sufficiently exposed to beauty and greatness?

I urge you—as one who has lived fairly long without doing many things I should have done and having done many things I should not have—I urge you to expose yourself to beauty and greatness wherein it may be found. It takes effort. You are young and have energy. It requires brains and judgment. You have both.

It may involve money. How can it be better invested? Michaelangelo, having carved the magnificent David from a misshapen block of marble, was asked: "How could you see that beautiful figure in that ugly stone?" and he said: "There is beauty and ugliness in everything. What comes out depends upon me." So be it. Expose yourself to beauty and greatness at whatever cost—beauty of music and art and nature and people. Oh, by all means, great people. You cannot always know what is great and good and worthy of memory and evaluation-but someone knows. See ye him.

Affectionately,

Dad

PS Remember the best is yet to come!

Epilogue

Life has been better because of my unconventional upside down thinking.

Realizing that different people and situations come in our lives and if we go contrary to their opinion and feeling on certain subjects it serves us well. Personal gut feeling is better for the desired results.

Even as an adolescent if there was a certain food I didn't want, place I did not want to go or people I didn't want to associate with, I would act as if I did and then sabotage it so not to have to repeat the experience. Reaching into young adulthood this thinking was a pilot for choices in personal and business matters. A friend of mine, for example, would always want to do, go and be exactly opposite of what I wanted. By attacking his frame of mind I would simply express what I didn't want to accomplish to accomplish what I wanted.

In business I violated the rule of selling insurance as an "investment," being told that I would fail—it had the opposite effect for forty years: Functioning as a one-man company helped me enormously from a psychological and financial viewpoint. Using professional services on a bartering basis to integrate into my mode of operandi.

I discovered how to get more from a dollar than most know how to do with ten dollars. It has been essential enabling me to make each $10,000 of income do the work of a much higher multiple. Discovering that the more money I saved the more money I had right now.

Legal and medical issues have become an avocation to untangle the enormous entanglement of idealism and righteousness. Both areas are subverted by other than altruistic means that demeans the client and kills the patient. My respect has diminished for these professions, which have been tainted because of the opportunistic individuals and casts an ominous warning.

Prior to my mother's death after being admitted to the hospital she stated that the white coats of the doctors intimidated her and she felt meek as a lamb. Conversely my feeling is the antithesis of this. Knowing that often the cure is the problem rather than the disease. After my mother's death, I asked her physician why he gave her so much of a certain drug (Lasix—which removed a lot of fluid from the lungs). His harsh reply was, "We threw everything on the shelf at her." Feelings of cold chills ran down my spine knowing this accelerated her demise. I have seen ignorance prevail in almost every aspect of life—from religion, business, law, and medicine. There have been some humorous, but tragic learning experiences about the human animal and how it thinks and reacts. Subtle childhood experiences thru what we see, hear and feel can have a remarkable influence on how our mind works. For example, the fascination of nurses I had as a child with their blue capes and white uniforms thrust me into a relationship that had far reaching results affecting many lives. It was the look and feel, as a child, that created this magnetic pull to experience in depth, which I had felt as a five year old with the two nurses dating my uncle. I had an unbelievable curiosity and fascination with his two girlfriends, which was the beginning of my waterloo. This seems like yesterday, not 60 years ago. Remembering how upset I was when told that my uncle was marrying my girlfriend the nurse. I think back to how indelible this experience was.

The mind is the last unexplored continent. In some ways you can prophesize your good fortune and your death, simply by focusing your thinking where you want to be and do. You can see it happening. A few years ago I had a dream, which is as clear as if it were yesterday. I pictured myself living to age 81—dying in the winter of my 81st year. A color photograph of our wedding was shown at the local drive-in theater. We are cutting the wedding cake with the caption, *How to have your cake and eat it too* seems now even more prophetic, as my life has unfolded, dodging silver bullets in my upside down thinking. Yes we are potentially capable of hypnotizing our self to enjoy life, dull pain, to expel fear and strengthen our resolve. To live our life with gusto, filling our moments with thought, action and filling the unforgiving minute with 60 minutes worth of distance run is a daunting task but a worthy one to complete the circle of living.

Acknowledgements from two dear friends, neither knowing the other, as presented on my 50th birthday:

"L" FOR DONALD—January 26, 1985

I

If Donald Patrick Foster were a dream
and not real flesh and blood, it would seem
that tales about him always should evoke
rejoinders such as, "surely, that's a joke!"
But jest I not, for facts are stranger here
Than fiction's wildest fancy could appear
(The joke's as old as Ireland's elfin eye,
the butt of which is Portsmouth, you and I.)

II

When Donald walks into a crowded room,
more noisy than the loudest sonic boom,
Forthwith our Don preempts both sound and space
And substitutes his presence in their place.
His modulating tones—both low and high,
His raucous laughter rising to the sky,
Are all devoured and relished word by word
as gospel, although palpably absurd.

III

His modesty of body as a child
was such his shy refinement felt defiled,
if team-mates saw him shower in the nude;
he wore his sweat-soaked drawers as less crude.
These puerile inhibitions, one suspects,
have not extended to the other sex—

the number of the flock that he has sired
bespeaks a man who's timely unattired.

IV
When bourbon, vodka, gin or even wine
are de rigueur, Don stands the first in line;
he orders "glasses round" and "fill the cup,"
when lesser topers have all given up.
His appetite for viands is as great;
the only rival to his cup, his plate—
such prodigies of hunger and or thirst,
one wonders why the hell he hasn't burst.

V
But Donald has his own Achille's heel—
his fatal fascination for the wheel.
With drink in hand he charges forth defiant—
where is the David who dare face this giant?
King of the Road—no license in his name—
no fault of his—the stupid law's to blame.
The judges nodded—listened with a smile.
We didn't see our Donald for a while.

VI
"Improbable," Unlikely," did you say?
What if I told you on this very day
that Donald Patrick Foster vaunts his glee
at having trounced his first half century,
and promises that two score years and ten
are but an appetizer to his yen.
We quake and shake and shudder at this vow

and scratch our hapless heads and wonder how.
But should time stop when he has just begun,
I'll bet my boots he'll go on having fun.

                Charles A. McDuffie

Ode to Donald Patrick Foster 1935–1985 and Beyond

I

Today Donald Patrick Foster turns fifty
Isn't it great? Isn't it nifty?
There are certainly some of us alive
Who never suspected he would survive.
So "mirabile dictue" let's all pause
To give this unique man our applause.

II

From the days when he was known as Fakey Foo Foo Foul Shot
He has experienced adventures of a varied and curious lot.
At the very beginning of his grandstand plan
He wisely chose a sidekick named Anne
As a helpmate she has proved to be beyond compare
She has had patience—she has had flair.

III

In his twenties he earned an auspicious label
As member of the Million Dollar Round Table.
Probably the youngest to bear such a name,
It brought him fortune. It brought him fame.

IV

Donald Patrick Foster became the pater noster
To a large vivacious clan.
Along the way he has been the weaver of
Many a clever circuitous plan.

V

He enjoys playing games of the mind
His musings are often of a philosophical kind.

VI

For Friday, his special day to celebrate,
He has made sacrifices small and great.
One of his continuing gestures resulted without bail
In an ill-ustrious stay in the Mecklenburg jail.

VII

Did his embarrassing stint begin to put a dent in his style?
Not for more than the shortest while.
A designated driver was added to his payroll
To make possible a weekly bourbon bowl.

VIII

Donald Patrick Foster
Of friends and foes he's got quite a roster
For folks and motions to analyze
As a pastime he highly does prize.

IX

And so on this his natal day
To the one-of-a-kind original
True homage we pay.

Fred and Bonnie Korta

0-595-28932-0

Printed in the United States
20957LVS00005B/331